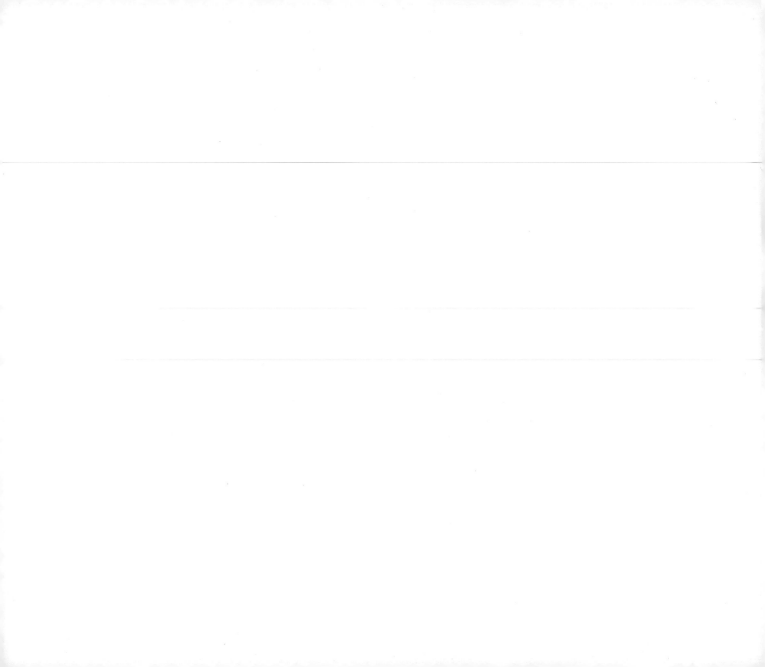

For the Love of
the CHICAGO
CUBS

Lew Freedman

WEST
SIDE
PUBLISHING

Lew Freedman is a Chicago-based sportswriter who has more than 250 journalism awards and 35 books to his credit. A graduate of Boston University, Freedman has a master's degree from Alaska Pacific University. He has worked on the staffs of the *Chicago Tribune*, the *Anchorage Daily News, The Philadelphia Inquirer*, and other newspapers. He and his wife Debra live in Bolingbrook, Illinois.

Contributing Writers: Jill Oldham and Marty Strasen

Factual verification by Karl Hente

ACKNOWLEDGMENTS

Lyrics from "Men in Blue" (pgs. 48 and 193) used with permission of YarMOUTH Publishing and ATHERITZ Music ©1984.

"Go Cubs Go" (pg. 96) written by Steve Goodman. Published by Big Ears Music, Inc. o/b/o itself & Red Pajamas Music (ASCAP). Lyrics reprinted with permission.

"The Cubbies Are Rockin'" (pg. 190) Words and music by Barry Goldberg and Aram Goldberg. Copyright ©1989 UNIVERSAL—SONGS OF POLY-GRAM INTERNATIONAL, INC. and BARRY GOLDBERG MUSIC. All rights administered by UNIVERSAL—SONGS OF POLYGRAM INTERNATIONAL, INC. International Copyright Secured. All Rights Reserved. Lyrics reprinted with permission.

"You're My Cubs" (pg. 238) Music & Lyrics by Alan Barcus, Old Harrier Music (ASCAP). Lyrics reprinted with permission.

Front cover: ©**Corbis** Warren Wimmer, (right); **Getty Images** (top left); MLB Photos (left center & bottom left)

Back cover: **Getty Images** (left); *Sports Illustrated* (right)

AP Images: 10, 11, 33, 63, 68, 74, 88, 99, 130, 145, 177 (left center), 180, 183, 213, 247; **Leo Bauby:** 66; **Pat Cabai:** 21; **Ken Carl, www.kencarl.com:** 225, 229; **Chicago History Museum:** *Chicago Daily News*, SDN-006880, 7, SDN-060448, 122, SDN-067251, 160, SDN-063316, 212, SDN-007034, 251; **Columbia Pictures:** 56 (top right); ©**Corbis:** 198 (bottom right); Bettmann, contents, 45, 49, 77, 86, 102, 116, 124, 125, 134, 201, 208, 237 (right); Mark Cowan/Icon SMI, 174; Laura Farr/ZUMA, 151 (left); Andrew Gombert/epa, 254; John Gress/Reuters, 98, 194, 282 (right); Tom Hood/epa, 280; Frank Jansly/Icon SMI, 196; Tannen Maury/epa, 55, 142; Neal Preston, 189; Reuters, 173; Joseph Sohm/Visions of America, 17, 108, 109 (left); Davis Turner/Reuters, 198 (bottom left); Underwood & Underwood, contents, 135, 141 (right), 172; John Zich/NewSport, 69; **Fotolia:** Alessandro Contadin, 245; **Getty Images:** contents, 5, 20, 26–27, 28, 42, 46 (bottom), 72, 73, 76, 79, 80, 83, 90, 92, 93, 95 (right), 96–97, 110, 119, 126–127, 131, 136, 137, 138, 144, 150, 151 (top right), 156, 162, 165, 166, 169, 177 (right center & bottom), 188 (right), 191, 192, 197, 198 (top left & top right), 211, 214, 216 (bottom left), 217, 220, 223, 231, 236 (left), 239, 240, 244, 248, 249, 253, 256, 260, 263, 270, 272, 278, 279, 283 (right); AFP, 9, 276; Diamond Images, 37, 44; MLB Photos, 12, 43, 85, 94 (right), 120, 128, 146, 148, 154, 186, 203, 216 (right), 222 (right), 241; Ronald C. Modra/Sports Imagery, 234; *Sports Illustrated*, 50, 91, 101, 109 (center), 113, 114, 129, 159, 222 (left), 274; Time Life Pictures, 31, 205, 255; **Bill Greenblatt:** 185; **iStockphoto:** 13; **Jennifer Huston Photography:** 178; **Compliments JDRF Illinois, David Blachman photographer:** 233; **Library of Congress:** 24, 54, 259; **National Baseball Hall of Fame Library, Cooperstown, NY:** 39, 67, 105; **NFL:** 151 (bottom right); **PhotoDisc:** 4, 40, 48, 51, 53, 57, 82, 181, 268, 269 (bottom); **PIL Collection:** contents, 8, 25, 34, 52, 64, 65, 84, 140 (left), 171, 193, 210, 219, 243, 262, 266, 269 (top); **SAD Memorabilia:** 18, 29, 30, 47, 58, 78, 89, 106, 115, 132, 143, 158, 161, 199 (top), 204, 224, 226, 238 (top), 275; **Shutterstock:** 6, 16, 36, 111, 121, 167, 168, 182, 246, 264, 271; **Stockbyte:** 199 (bottom); **Twentieth Century Fox:** 56 (bottom left); **Universal Pictures:** 56 (top left & bottom right); **WireImage:** 19; **ZUMA Press:** Cal Sport Media, 149; Charles M. Conlon, 38; Albert Dickson/*Sporting News*, 71; Jay Drowns/TSN, 59; Jerry Lai/USP, 60–61; *Sporting News*, 22, 35, 107, 123, 153, 216 (top left)

Contributing Illustrator: Elizabeth Traynor

Photography: PDR Productions, Inc./Peter Rossi

West Side Publishing is a division of Publications International, Ltd.

ISBN-13: 978-1-4127-1599-7
ISBN-10: 1-4127-1599-7

Manufactured in China.

8 7 6 5 4 3 2 1

Library of Congress Control Number: 2008931656

ers Hornsby

Billy Williams

CONTENTS

CHAPTER ONE

"TAKE ME OUT TO THE BALL GAME" • 4

CHAPTER TWO

"MEN IN BLUE" • 48

CHAPTER THREE

"GO CUBS GO" • 96

CHAPTER FOUR

"THE GLORY OF THE CUBS" • 142

CHAPTER FIVE

"THE CUBBIES ARE ROCKIN'" • 190

CHAPTER SIX

"YOU'RE MY CUBS" • 238

INDEX • 284

k DeRosa

Stan Hack

"TAKE ME OUT TO THE BALL GAME"

"Take me out to the ball game,

Take me out with the crowd.

Buy me some peanuts and Cracker Jack,

I don't care if I never get back."

—LYRICS BY JACK NORWORTH, 1908

"It's a great day for a ball game.
Let's play two!"

—ERNIE BANKS, CUBS HALL OF FAME SHORTSTOP AND FIRST BASEMAN

WHAT'S IN A NAME?

Although the Cubs are the only original National League team still playing in their city of origin, the ballclub—like many during the formative years from 1876 to 1901—underwent a series of name changes. In fact, Chicago's National League ballclub had three "official" names during its first 30 years of existence. They were first known as the White Stockings (not to be confused with the American League's White Sox, who were formed in 1900) and then the Colts, before becoming the Cubs in 1902. Some of the team's unofficial names include the Black Stockings, the Rough Riders, the Rainmakers, the Remnants, and the Orphans, so named after longtime player-manager Cap Anson departed after the 1897 season.

More often than not in 1908, and most other years in the early 20th century, the Cubs walked off the field at West Side Grounds (and every other park) as winners.

BASEBALL'S FAVORITE SONG

It never won a Grammy or an Academy Award or was featured on an American Top 40 list, but "Take Me Out to the Ball Game" is one of the most popular songs in American history, judging by the number of people who sing it in public without being forced to do so. Polls list "Take Me Out to the Ball Game" as the third most recognized song in America, after "Happy Birthday" and "The Star-Spangled Banner."

Some 78 million people attended major-league baseball games in 2008, more than 3 million of them at Wrigley Field, and millions more attended minor-league games. Standing up and singing "Take Me Out to the Ball Game" in the middle of the seventh inning to stretch one's muscles is a ritual common to nearly every park. Fans sing with gusto (and often out of key) because it's a tradition and it's fun to do.

Ironically, the song was written by two men who had never even seen a baseball game. Jack Norworth wrote the words in 1908, and Albert Von Tilzer added the music. While riding the subway in New York City, Norworth saw a poster advertising "Baseball Today" at the Polo Grounds. Inspired by the sign, he scrawled out the lyrics on the back of an envelope. "Take Me Out to the Ball Game" has persevered in American culture ever since.

All baseball fans claim kinship with "Take Me Out to the Ball Game," which is now considered the unofficial anthem of the sport, but at Wrigley Field, the singing of the song has been elevated to an art form. Credit broadcaster Harry Caray for that.

THE SENSATIONAL BASE BALL SONG

TAKE ME OUT TO THE BALL GAME

WORDS BY JACK NORWORTH
MUSIC BY ALBERT VON TILZER

THE YORK MUSIC CO
213 WEST 28TH ST. N.Y.

5

Caray had been calling games for decades before he arrived on the north side of the Windy City in 1982. In 1976, while Caray was working for the White Sox, team owner Bill Veeck overheard him singing "Take Me Out to the Ball Game" to himself during the seventh-inning stretch. After that, Veeck encouraged the crooner to lead sing-alongs with the fans.

By the time he transferred his act across town six years later, Caray had perfected his role as seventh-inning stretch conductor. He was a white-haired orchestra leader, leaning out of the open window of the press box high above home plate, swinging his microphone like a baton, and leading the masses in making music. It made for a memorable sight and was one of the special things about going to a game at Wrigley Field. You got a baseball game and a septuagenarian songbird all for the same ticket price.

The routine became so popular that even disheartened Cubs fans, who were inclined to leave early because their team was getting clob-bered (and those occasions were common some years), stuck around long enough to experience the sing-along before heading for the El train.

And while Harry was recuperating from a stroke in 1987, and then after he died in 1998, the Cubs kept the tradition going with special guests. Caray may have been a unique character, soaking in the adulation as much as any ham of a performer, but he also would have recognized that the show must go on. The singer of the day might be an old Cub favorite, an actor, a politician, or a comedian.

Harry Caray

Shabby vocal chords might prevent them from carrying a tune or keeping the tempo, but the 40,000 fans in the stands always get it right.

THE COMEBACK KIDS

On September 12 and September 13, 1998, the Cubs benefited from a baseball rarity—**dramatic come-from-behind victories two days in a row against the same team.** In the first game, the Cubs were down 12–10 going into the bottom of the ninth. The Cubs tied it up with back-to-back singles by Sammy Sosa and Glenallen Hill, a sacrifice bunt by Gary Gaetti, and a two-run single by Tyler Houston. Mickey Morandini took a walk, then with two men on, Orlando Merced hit a walk-off homer to knock out the Milwaukee Brewers 15–12. The next day, the Cubs squandered a three-run eighth-inning lead, only to come back and tie it in the bottom of the ninth. With the score tied 10–10 in the bottom of the tenth, Mark Grace hit a solo shot to deep right field to win the ball game 11–10.

"I'm going to savor the hell out of this moment."

—Cubs outfielder Keith Moreland in 1984, after the team reached the postseason for the first time in 39 years

Rick Sutcliffe and Ryne Sandberg celebrate after the Cubs clinched the NL East on September 24, 1984.

MAJOR LEAGUE TOTALS				
G	W	L	SO	ERA
451	174	150	1,601	3.49

KEN HOLTZMAN: CHICAGO'S SANDY KOUFAX

Young Ken Holtzman often drew comparisons to Sandy Koufax, mostly because he was left-handed, Jewish, and broke into the majors in 1965, when the Dodger hurler was at the peak of his national fame.

Yet in Holtzman's mind, he was just the "other" Jewish pitcher. As a rookie, the only thing Holtzman felt he had in common with Koufax was that they both attended synagogue on the high holidays. Koufax, in fact, was such a hero to Jewish Americans that Holtzman's own mother reportedly had trouble deciding whom to root for when the two pitchers faced each other.

Holtzman did show flashes of brilliance throughout his career, the most notable being a pair of no-hitters thrown for the Cubs before he turned 25. The first came in August of '69 against the Atlanta Braves at Wrigley Field—a feat Holtzman achieved, amazingly, without recording a single strikeout. Jubilant fans swarmed the field after the 3–0 victory that kept the Cubs eight games ahead of the Mets in the NL East—at least for a little while longer. The second no-no came in June of '71, this time with a 1–0 victory over the Cincinnati Reds.

Despite these unforgettable perfor-mances, 54 complete games, and more than a dozen shutouts, Holtzman was traded at the end of the '71 season. Over his 15-year career, Holtzman was elected to the All-Star team twice, but never while with the Cubs. He returned to Chicago for the last year of his career, and, although his skills were all but gone, fans cheered the popular pitcher's homecoming.

> Holtzman remains the only Cubs pitcher since 1900 to throw more than one no-hitter.

THE CURSE
OF THE BILLY GOAT

Life would have been a lot easier for everyone if old William "Billy Goat" Sianis owned a goldfish or a talkative parrot—a pet that could not easily be led into Wrigley Field on a leash. But no, his faithful sidekick was a companionable goat named Murphy that was a walking, breathing, albeit smelly, symbol of his business.

It was not as if the proprietor of the Billy Goat Tavern was trying to be chintzy. He paid $7.20 for the goat to be properly admitted to Wrigley Field on that fateful October 6 during the 1945 World Series against the Detroit Tigers. And it wasn't as if he was an irresponsible parent letting his kid run wild through the concourses.

Heck, the goat was on a leash! And somehow, Sianis and Murphy even finagled their way onto the playing field, where the animal was paraded around, proudly displaying a blanket featuring the words "We Got Detroit's Goat."

Up until then, everyone was on the same side. But after that cameo on the grass, Cubs owner P. K. Wrigley ordered security to give the goat the heave-ho when it started to rain, proclaiming, "The goat stinks." Those were fighting words to an insulted Sianis, and he fought back with other words. Infamously, he put a curse on the Cubs, saying the team would never win a world championship again. After the Cubs lost the 1945 World Series to the Tigers, Sianis sent a note to P. K. Wrigley that simply stated, "Who stinks now?"

Sianis knew how to hold a grudge. For nearly 24 years, he stood by the hex, refusing to lift it. Finally, in 1969, the year before he passed away, Sianis revoked the curse, but apparently by then it was out of his hands because we all know how the '69 season ended for the North Siders.

The Cubs have been trying to undo the curse since 1945. Not only have they not won a World Series in that time frame, they haven't even *reached* the fall classic since then. Future generations of Sianises, as well as offspring of the mystical goat, have put forth good-faith efforts to lift the plague on the Cubs. Several times, William Sianis's nephew Sam has brought a descendant of Murphy to the park in an effort to eradicate the curse. In 1998, after Sam paraded a goat around the field, he stated that he'd done his part, and the rest was up to the Cubs.

Yet the Cubs still haven't put together the proper formula to trump the original fiery words. Do the Cubs need to hire a witch doctor to remove the curse? Do they need to fill the park to capacity with goats for one game? Should the team drink a toast with goat's milk in the club-

Former manager Dusty Baker was a skeptic. He didn't believe in no stinkin' curses. And what happened to Dusty? He was run out of town. Entering the 2009 season, the goat was still undefeated, symbolizing a century's worth of futility.

house before each game? Would it be a sign if the Cubs could ferret out a choice young player whose last name is Goat? Or perhaps the Cubs simply need to adopt a goat as their mascot?

And what became of the Billy Goat Tavern? Its fortunes seem to have turned 180 degrees from those of the Cubs. The subject of humorous skits on *Saturday Night Live* is thriving as never before, with busloads of tourists pulling up to eat cheezborgers and cheeps (no fries), and it has added several Chicagoland locations.

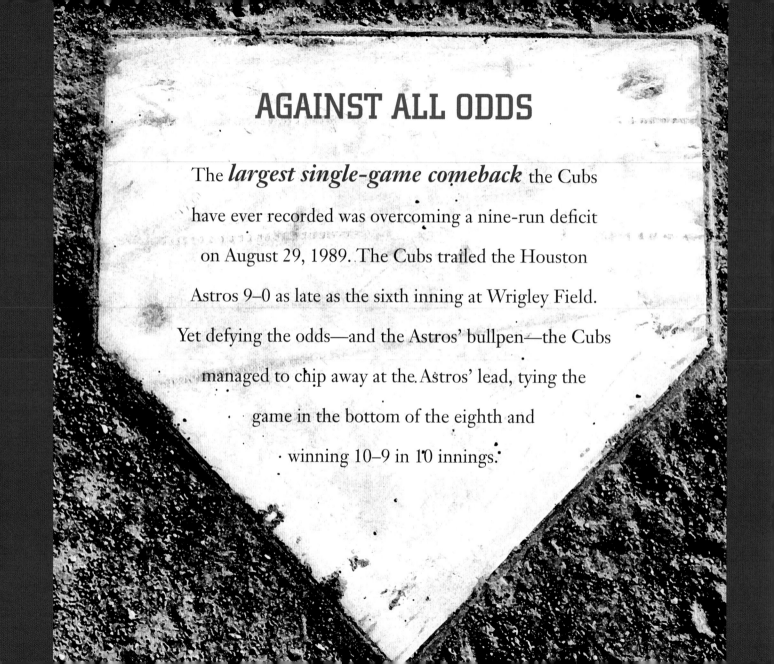

AGAINST ALL ODDS

The ***largest single-game comeback*** the Cubs have ever recorded was overcoming a nine-run deficit on August 29, 1989. The Cubs trailed the Houston Astros 9–0 as late as the sixth inning at Wrigley Field. Yet defying the odds—and the Astros' bullpen—the Cubs managed to chip away at the Astros' lead, tying the game in the bottom of the eighth and winning 10–9 in 10 innings.

"Every player should be accorded the privilege of at least one season with the Chicago Cubs. That's baseball as it should be played—in God's own sunshine. And that's really living."

— ALVIN DARK, FORMER CUBS PLAYER AND COACH

MR. CUB: ERNIE BANKS

Ernie Banks likes to wear bow ties, and he thinks every man should. Ernie Banks likes to eat sushi, and he thinks everyone should. Ernie Banks thinks every man should have a wife to love because he is a hopeless romantic.

If you disagree with him on any of these personal policies, he'll genially and graciously engage you in a debate about why you are wrong, but always with a smile on his face. In retirement, "Mr. Cub"—one of the most popular players in Cubs history—has a lot more on his mind than baseball. It is his daily mission to put a smile on the face of everyone he meets. One of the nicest and most genuine human beings you'll ever meet,

Hall of Famer Banks is also one of the sunniest ambassadors baseball has ever had.

The early 1950s were not an opportune time to be a black man in the United States. Emerging from a financially deprived upbringing in Dallas, Texas, the teenaged Banks starred with the Kansas City Monarchs, one of the last vestiges of greatness in the fading Negro Leagues. The Monarchs' much-admired and knowledgeable manager, Buck O'Neil, took Banks under his wing and taught him everything from how to be patient at the plate to how to cope with a racist society before shipping him off to the Cubs. Banks says he gained his positive outlook from playing under O'Neil.

The maturity Banks picked up in the Negro Leagues helped him as he became the Cubs' first black player, and when he was joined by his friend, second baseman Gene Baker, the duo became the first black double-play combo in

MAJOR LEAGUE TOTALS			
G	HR	RBI	BA
2,528	512	1,636	.274

the majors. From there, Banks quickly rose to stardom, leading the league in total home runs in 1958 and 1960 and earning MVP honors twice, in 1958 and '59. He stroked 512 homers throughout his storied career with the Cubs, five times hitting 40 or more in a season.

A shortstop for almost a decade—and a seven-time All-Star during those years—Banks moved to first base in 1962, where he was named an All-Star four more times. At first base, he became the senior man in a top-notch infield featuring Ron Santo at third, Don Kessinger at short, and Glenn Beckert at second.

The always-optimistic Banks never allowed the Cubs' on-field record to dent his positive demeanor. Banks was the ultimate "We'll get 'em tomorrow" guy. Each spring he predicted the Cubs would win the pennant, and each autumn he was disappointed. But every year he again predicted that the next season would be the Cubs' turn, and he put his heart and his formidable skills into every game, joyfully exhorting "Let's

play two" every chance he got.

Banks's attitude made him a beloved figure to Cubs fans when he played, and he has maintained that stature since he retired. One need only look to the left-field foul pole at Wrigley Field, where a flag bearing his retired jersey No. 14 waves proudly in the breeze, and to the commemorative statue that stands in prominence outside the park to see what Mr. Cub has meant to the franchise.

2008 CUBS HIGHLIGHTS

The 2008 regular season was loaded with highlights for the Chicago Cubs and their fans—from start to finish. Here are some of the best:

March 31—Kosuke Fukudome ties the season opener with the visiting Brewers on a three-run, ninth-inning homer in his major-league debut.

May 19—**Geovany Soto** becomes the first Cubs catcher in 49 years to hit an inside-the-park home run when he chugs around the bases in a 7–2 win at Houston.

May 30—Down 9–1 after five innings, the Cubs score nine unanswered runs to pull out a stunning 10–9 victory over the Colorado Rockies at Wrigley Field.

June 20—Aramis Ramirez hits two home runs, including a walk-off winner, as the Cubs kick off a crosstown sweep of the White Sox.

June 30 and August 6—Mark DeRosa slugs grand slams against the Giants and Astros, respectively, the third and fourth of his career. The latter, at Wrigley, led to his first career "curtain call."

July 13—The Cubs tie the NL record of eight players selected for the All-Star Game when Carlos Marmol is named to replace injured teammate Kerry Wood on the roster. He joins teammates Geovany Soto, Alfonso Soriano, Kosuke Fukudome, Ryan Dempster, Carlos Zambrano, and Aramis Ramirez.

July 28–31—In a crucial four-game series between division title contenders, the Cubs sweep the Brewers in dominant fashion at Miller Park. Chicago outscores Milwaukee 31–11 and ends the series with a five-game lead in the NL Central.

August 8—Henry Blanco smacks an 11th-inning, walk-off single as the cardiac Cubs finish another thrilling comeback to notch a 3–2 victory over the rival Cardinals.

August 15—The Cubs post their 35th come-from-behind win of the season when, with one out in the ninth, pinch-hitter Daryle Ward drills a three-run homer to put the Cubs ahead of the Marlins. They go on to win 6–5.

September 14—Carlos Zambrano becomes the first Cubs pitcher in 36 years to throw a no-hitter. He does so with 10 strikeouts and one walk against the Astros in a game moved to Milwaukee because of Hurricane Ike.

September 15—Ted Lilly and the Cubs' bullpen follow Big Z's no-no with a one-hitter over the Astros, holding them hitless through six frames. It's the first time in major-league history that a team follows a no-hitter with a one-hitter.

September 17—At the request of Hall of Famer Ernie Banks, Pearl Jam lead singer, Chicago native, and lifelong Cubs fan Eddie Vedder releases a song for his favorite team entitled, "All the Way."

September 18—Trailing the Brewers 6–2 with two outs in the bottom of the ninth, the Cubs—thanks in part to a three-run homer by Geovany Soto—rally for four runs to tie it, then win it in the 12th on Derrek Lee's walk-off single.

September 20—The Cubs clinch their second straight NL Central title with a 5–4 victory over the Cardinals at Wrigley Field.

BUCK O'NEIL

Even in his nineties, Buck O'Neil maintained an iron handshake and a bass voice almost as deep as that of actor James Earl Jones. Most of the gregarious O'Neil's baseball life took place out of the limelight because most of it was confined to the Negro Leagues during the 1930s and '40s, when Major League Baseball banned all African Americans. Nevertheless, the dapper-dressing O'Neil answered segregation by dining in the finest black-owned restaurants and by staying in the finest black-owned hotels. Ignoring societal constraints as best as possible, he made sure he genuinely enjoyed life.

O'Neil was an excellent fielding first baseman, who also won batting titles for the Monarchs in 1940 and '46. He was an **astute manager who ruled with considered judgment rather than explosive instinct.** When his beloved Kansas City Monarchs devolved into a mere barnstorming team in the mid-1950s, O'Neil officially became a scout for the Cubs, and then, in 1962, **the first uniformed black coach in major-league history** as part of the College of Coaches.

Both mentor and friend, O'Neil had tight relationships with Hall of Famers Ernie Banks and Billy Williams, who sometimes needed a guiding hand from an older black man who had seen more of life. A driving force in the creation of the Negro Leagues Baseball Museum in Kansas City and a spokesman for many African American stars who predeceased him, O'Neil experienced a renaissance in public life when documentary filmmaker Ken Burns featured him in his 1994 opus *Baseball*. Most baseball fans believe that O'Neil, who died in 2006, should be enshrined in the Baseball Hall of Fame in Cooperstown, New York.

ALBERT SPALDING

Albert Goodwill Spalding was born in Byron, Illinois, in 1850. He was an exemplary pitcher—the best of his time—but most of his hurling was done in the 1860s and '70s, before the National League, an organization he helped create, was formed in 1876. Anxious to begin a new career in the business world, Spalding was persuaded to play one last season for the league's fledgling Chicago franchise and posted a record of 47–12 with an astounding 1.75 ERA.

In an era when pitchers finished what they started unless a barrage of runs cascaded upon them, Spalding still stood out with 60 complete games in 61 starts during that lone season he played for Chicago. Macho stubbornness notwithstanding, Spalding believed it was foolish for fielders to attempt to catch batted balls barehanded. So, that year when he took the mound, Spalding—although ridiculed by some—became the first star player to wear a glove in the field for protection.

In 1876, Spalding and his brother invested $800 to open their first sporting goods store in Chicago. The shop grew into the largest sporting goods company in America, and Spalding made more money from that venture than from playing baseball. In 1877, the foresighted Spalding published the first baseball rules booklet, followed by an annual publication that he called *Spalding's Official Baseball Guide*. He later served as the team's secretary (general manager) and team president. He even led a group of National League players on a barnstorming tour around the world and made an attempt, albeit unsuccessfully, to bring night baseball to Chicago.

"*Professional baseball is on the wane. Salaries must come down or the interest of the public must be increased in some way. If one or the other does not happen, bankruptcy stares every team in the face.*"

—ALBERT SPALDING, 1881

"I didn't play the game right because I saw a reward at the end of the tunnel. I played it right because that's what you're supposed to do—play it right and with respect."

—RYNE SANDBERG, FROM HIS HALL OF FAME INDUCTION SPEECH IN 2005

AWESOME DAWSON

The unlikely story of how the power-hitting, fan-favorite Andre Dawson became a Cub is etched in club lore. Already a proven star with the Montreal Expos, Dawson became a free agent after the 1986 season, but some teams fretted about hiring him because of his creaky knees.

Quite conscious of the aggravation his knees had caused and concerned about his future, Dawson did not take a greedy outlook into free agency. He carefully considered his options and decided that the Cubs and Wrigley Field provided his smartest option. Wrigley had a grass outfield that would be gentler on his knees than an artificial turf surface.

At first the aloof Cubs ignored Dawson's overtures to join the club. Alarmed, Dawson practically had to beg to join the team, presenting a blank contract to team officials. The Cubs filled it out for $500,000, with incentives worth an additional $250,000. No one imagined the bargain Dawson would turn out to be during the 1987 season as he clubbed 49 home runs with 137 RBI and became such a feared figure at the plate that he won the Most Valuable Player Award for a last-place team. He also hit for the cycle in April and earned a seventh Gold Glove Award that season. Given his pay rate, his success was almost embarrassing to the team.

Nicknamed "The Hawk," Dawson was a slick fielder who, despite his aching knees, managed to snag fly balls that seemed out of reach. In a career that spanned 21 seasons in the majors, he was one of baseball's best all-around players—hitting for power and average while providing speed on the bases and stellar defense in right field. He spent six years with the Cubs and was an All-Star five of them. Dawson's professionalism, hustle, and productivity made him much-admired by the Wrigley Field cognoscenti, especially fans in the right-field bleachers, who adopted the moniker "Andre's Army" and would bow to their fearless leader to show their respect and gratitude after he'd made a spectacular play.

Dawson is **one of only a handful of players to record more than 300 home runs and 300 stolen bases in his major-league career.** And although he joined the Marlins' front office after his retirement in 1996 (he finally earned a World Series ring in 2003 after they bested the Cubs in the NLCS and the Yankees in the fall classic), he still remains a favorite in the hearts of Cubs fans.

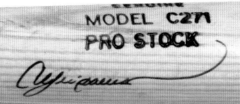

THE COLLEGE OF
COACHES

The notion of turning over field leadership of the Cubs to **a rotating group of coaches** rather than having a permanently installed manager is regarded as perhaps the top-ranked harebrained scheme in major-league history. The endeavor was nicknamed "The College of Coaches," but, in the end, it flunked out.

The idea whose time had not yet come was instituted by Cubs owner P. K. Wrigley for the 1961 season and lasted through the 1962 season, which was about two years too long for most of the players and fans.

"Heavens," Wrigley said, in rationalizing his idea to dump the manager title, "we don't need a dictator."

This unintentionally pithy comment ignored the fact that all baseball teams had operated under the one-leader, one-voice rule since the birth of the sport. The best example of committee leadership anyone could find was Congress, and that wasn't terribly encouraging.

During the original spin of the wheel of fortune, there were eight coaches in the mix (though more were added later), but the head coach role was not equally shared. Vedie Himsl, Harry Craft, Elvin Tappe, and Lou Klein took turns being head coach in 1961. Tappe, Klein, and Charlie Metro took turns in 1962.

The situation was chaotic to say the least. The team was bad, and nobody believed Ernie Banks for a second when he said, "The Cubs are due in '62." In 1963, although Wrigley did not officially bring back the manager title, he appointed Bob Kennedy head coach, a role he served until mid-1965.

They may be smiling here, but by the end of the '62 season the men who participated in the ill-fated "College of Coaches" were bemoaning their part in the foolish experiment.

RONNIE "WOO-WOO" WICKERS

It's not as if he invented the expression "Woo-Woo," but Ronnie Wickers, **unofficial Cubs mascot,** doesn't need a patent. Perhaps the most enthusiastic Cubs fan there is, Wickers is also the team's most identifiable supporter, someone always at Wrigley Field on game days. And after decades of dressing the part of No. 1 Cubs fan, the outgoing, passionate Wickers is now as much a part of the Wrigley scene as the ivy and the manual scoreboard.

Despite frequent home game sellouts, Ronnie finds a way into the Friendly Confines.

> ## "He's a warm individual and he's been through a lot."
>
> —PAUL HOFFMAN, DOCUMENTARY FILMMAKER, SPEAKING ABOUT RONNIE WOO-WOO

Sometimes he purchases his own ticket, washing windows and doing odd jobs for local businesses to earn money. Often, however, friendly fans who recognize Wickers outside the ballpark give him a ticket to enjoy the game and pump up the crowd with his signature style.

Each and every game day (and most off days, too) he sports a full Cubs uniform—including a cap, stirrups, and batting gloves—and brings along his vocal "talents" as well. For more than five decades, his voice has echoed from all corners of the ballpark and throughout Wrigleyville: "Woo! Cubs! Woo! Ernie! Woo! Ryno! Woo! Zambrano! Woo!..." You get the picture.

Why Woo?

"It just came to me," Wickers said of his trademark expression. Ronnie, who was born in

1941 and was raised by his grandmother, began "woo"ing in the late 1950s. He once said he could woo for six hours nonstop because he never got tired. Perhaps it was this relentlessness that led Harry Caray to nickname him "Leather Lungs."

Season after season, game after game finds him dressed in uniform, cap on head, with a smile on his face and a chant at the ready. He attends every home game he can; at one time, he worked night jobs so he could go to day games. Another time in his life found him homeless and struggling with alcoholism, but he credits the lessons of baseball and his love of the Cubs for helping him turn his life around.

And his enthusiasm definitely has not gone unnoticed—by Cubs fans, Cubs players, even Cubs management. **In 2001, Wickers realized a lifelong dream when he was asked to lead the seventh-inning stretch—the first regular Cubs fan to do so.** After tearing up with emotion at the start, Ronnie pulled it together with "A-One! Woo! A-Two! Woo! A-Three! Woo!"

Cubs fan are divided in their feelings toward him. Some look at the superfan and see a guy with a few screws loose; others greet him with shouts of welcome and goodwill. Either way, the "woos" continue to ring throughout Wrigleyville, just as they have for the past 50 years.

HACK WILSON: SHORT BUT NOT SO SWEET

Lewis "Hack" Wilson was no hack, but his cracks of the bat were extraordinarily powerful.

Wilson had the squat body of an Olympic weight lifter, but his athletic specialty was quite different. Wilson, who stood 5′6″ but weighed 195 pounds, had an 18-inch neck (only slightly smaller than a supermodel's waist), huge arms, a barrel of an upper torso, and tree-trunklike thighs that tapered down to tiny feet. Unfortunately, his career was as compact as his size, partially due to his addiction to alcohol. There is no doubt that the frequency of Wilson's imbibing shortened both his baseball career and his life, which ended at age 48.

But when he laid off the spirits, Wilson was magnificent, an animal of a hitter who attacked the ball with teeth bared and determination advertised in his tense batting stance. When his timing was right, it was as if Wilson took a sledgehammer to the ball instead of a Louis-ville Slugger. **For one glorious season in 1930,** Wilson, a future Hall of Famer, was the best hitter of them all while playing outfield for the Cubs. That year **he batted .356, smashed 56 home runs**—a National League record that lasted until 1998—**and drove in 191 runs,** a single-season RBI record that still stands.

Hack Wilson

"*I never saw Wilson unfit to play. Hungover, yes, but never not ready to hit.*"

—FORMER CUBS MANAGER CHARLIE GRIMM

THE 1930s
THE DECADE OF THE CUBS

By now, most people are aware that the Cubs have not won a World Series since 1908. But the rest of the 20th century was not entirely an exercise in futility. In fact, many consider the **1930s the Golden Era of the Chicago Cubs.** Although they were unable to secure a world title, the Cubs did advance to the Series in 1932, 1935, and 1938 (and 1929 as well). As such, fans came to rely on the Cubs vying for world dominance every three years.

Players and fans of the 1930s-era Cubs didn't know how good they had it. Modern-day fans, ravenous for a World Series title, would feel blessed to have their team make such regular appearances in the final showdown. Even the two worst Cubs teams of the decade (1931 and 1939) each finished 84–70. Oh, to have such problems now!

Many attribute the success of the Cubs during this time to **a talented roster decorated with some of the best players in franchise history,** including Hack Wilson, Charlie Root, Gabby Hartnett, Rogers Hornsby, Charlie Grimm, Billy Herman, Stan Hack, Billy Jurges, Riggs Stephenson, Bill Lee, and Kiki Cuyler.

When Cubs owner William Wrigley, Jr., passed away in January 1932, his son P. K. took the reins. The change in stewardship seemed to have no effect on the team as the Cubs got off to a 22–9 start. The team finished 90–64 on the shoulders of pitcher Lon Warneke, who won 22 games, second baseman Billy Herman, who hit .314, and player-manager Charlie Grimm, who batted .307 with 80 clutch RBI.

Cubs Records of the 1930s
1930: 90–64; 1931: 84–70; 1932: 90–64; 1933: 86–68; 1934: 86–65; 1935: 100–54; 1936: 87–67; 1937: 93–61; 1938: 89–63; 1939: 84–70

The season culminated with a World Series confrontation against the Yankees, forever highlighted by Babe Ruth's "called shot" during the fifth inning of Game 3. As Wrigley fans razzed Ruth, he raised a finger each time Root earned a strike on him, as if to say, "That's one.... That's two." We'll never know if Ruth was raising a finger to say he had one more strike coming or if he was pointing to the outfield fence to indicate that's where the next pitch was headed. Regardless, he did hit Root's next pitch for a home run, and the Yankees went on to win the Series.

If ever the Cubs seemed destined to win the World Series, 1935 was the year. Although they were 10½ games out of first place in July, the Cubs went on a tear in the last month of the season, winning 21 straight games in September to finish 100–54. The Cubs appeared to have terrific momentum going into the Series, but they lost to the Detroit Tigers in six games.

After finishing second in 1936 and '37, the '38 Cubs were bouncing between third and fourth place for much of the season. As late as August 20, they trailed the first-place Pittsburgh Pirates by nine games, but once again, they put together a fabulous stretch run to claim the National League pennant. A notable victory was Gabby Hartnett's bottom-of-the-ninth, game-winning "Homer in the Gloamin'" under darkening skies on September 28. The win propelled the Cubs into first place, where they stayed for the remainder of the season. A date with the Yankees awaited the Cubs in the World Series. However, victory was not in the cards for the North Siders, as the Bronx Bombers barely broke a sweat in sweeping them four games to none to claim the world championship.

After that, Cubs pennants were few and far between.

ROGERS HORNSBY: THE RAJAH

Some say Rogers Hornsby was **the greatest right-handed hitter of all-time.** With seven batting titles and a lifetime batting average of .358, he certainly merits consideration. Throughout his remarkable career (1915–1937), Hornsby posted a batting average above .400 three times and set a post-1900 major-league record with a .424 batting average in 1924—a record that has stood for more than 80 years.

Hornsby, who played for the Cubs from 1929 to 1932, was a key figure in securing the '29 pennant when he batted .380, belted 39 homers, and drove in 149 runs. He succeeded Joe McCarthy as player-manager late

ROGERS HORNSBY
NATIONAL LEAGUE BATTING CHAMPION
7 YEARS - 1920 TO 1925; 1928. LIFETIME
BATTING AVERAGE .358 HIGHEST IN
NATIONAL LEAGUE HISTORY. HIT .424 IN
1924, 20TH CENTURY MAJOR LEAGUE RECORD.
MANAGER 1926 WORLD CHAMPION ST. LOUIS
CARDINALS. MOST-VALUABLE-PLAYER
1925 AND 1929.

in the 1930 season, but his **abrasive personality and impatience did not endear him to the team.** Hornsby was such a perfectionist that he frequently berated his players. He also avoided reading and watching movies because he believed they would weaken his eyesight and, therefore, his hitting prowess.

Hornsby went to the St. Louis Browns in 1933. Perhaps the marriage between him and the Cubs would have lasted longer if he had never assumed a managerial role. Still, there was no denying his earlier greatness on the field and at the plate, and he was elected to the Hall of Fame in 1942.

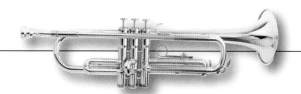

MAKING MUSIC AT THE FRIENDLY CONFINES

One tradition that has been in place for several years is that, on any given game day, **the Cubs' Dixieland Band entertains the crowd gathered at Wrigley Field.** They bellow out tunes outside the Friendly Confines before the game and then inside the park between innings. Dressed in full Cubs regalia—complete with Cubs jerseys and hats—the band, which includes horns, a clarinet, and even a banjo, is part of the nostalgia that makes a trip to Wrigley Field so special.

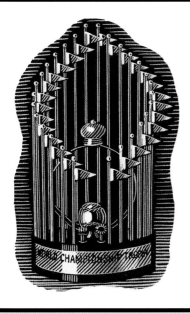

"No doubt, you get the feel[ing] that if you can win one pennant, you can do it again."

—LENNIE MERULLO, MEMBER OF THE 1945 PENNANT-WINNING CUBS

HEY! HEY! IT'S JACK BRICKHOUSE

In the heart of Chicago's legendary Magnificent Mile stands a statue of a Chicago legend. Hey, hey! That's famed sports broadcaster Jack Brickhouse, who, throughout a career spanning more than 40 years, would be identified with both the Chicago Cubs and the Chicago White Sox.

The man behind the voice first claimed a piece of the radio airwaves in 1934, but it wasn't until 1940 that he linked up with powerhouse WGN for the first time. And except for a few years when he took his words for hire elsewhere and a year serving as a marine in World War II, Brickhouse stayed at WGN's spot on the dial full-time until his retirement in 1981.

When he returned to Chicago in 1945 after his military service, Brickhouse didn't go back to WGN immediately. Instead, he spent that year broadcasting White Sox games for channel WJJD. And we all know what happened in 1945. Brickhouse missed out on calling the Cubs' spectacular World Series run—an opportunity that never came his way again.

Although he will forever be identified with baseball, the multitalented Brickhouse took a shot at describing any sport that came his way, from basketball to football and even wrestling. Over the years he also covered more than a few political and historical events, including reports from Saigon during the Vietnam War, Winston Churchill's funeral, and a papal audience with Pope Paul VI. Brickhouse won dozens of local and international awards throughout his multifaceted career.

But sports fans—especially Chicago sports fans—know he specialized in baseball. With a relaxed, easy style and genuine enthusiasm, Brickhouse made sure he brought listeners in on the action without taking attention away from the play, especially after games started airing on WGN TV in 1948.

Regular listeners recognized Brickhouse's trademark home-run call, which he came by accidentally. When a Cubs player socked a ball into orbit, he started yelling, "Hey! Hey!" But he was unaware he was using the phrase repeatedly until technicians played back his calls. Realizing it had a ring to it, he adopted it as his signature call.

After broadcasting more than 5,000 White Sox and Cubs games and calling "Hey! Hey!" more times than anyone could count, Brickhouse retired in 1981, a member of the broadcasters' wing of the Baseball Hall of Fame and the Radio Hall of Fame. The iconic announcer died in 1998, just months after the passing of another Chicago broadcasting legend, Harry Caray.

The Cubs have ensured that Brickhouse's voice will always be remembered by his fans, who can see his trademark "Hey! Hey!" painted on the foul poles at Wrigley Field.

MAJOR LEAGUE TOTALS			
G	HR	RBI	BA
1,852	213	976	.285

HANDY ANDY PAFKO

Although Andy Pafko, five-time All-Star and old-school gentleman, is happy to open doors for women, during his playing days, he slammed them in opponents' faces courtesy of his powerful bat and his sure-handed glove. Nicknamed "Handy Andy," Pafko was **one of the key offensive weapons on the famed 1945 NL pennant-winning team.** With a .298 average and 110 RBI that season—not to mention his National League-leading .995 fielding percentage—he powered the Cubs to the fall classic.

The popular Pafko would have preferred to remain with the Cubs for his entire career, but management traded him to the Dodgers in 1951. He bagged a world championship with the Milwaukee Braves in '57 before retiring from the game in 1959. The affable Pafko continued his career in baseball, serving as a major-league coach, minor-league manager, and then a scout, spending more than 40 years in the game.

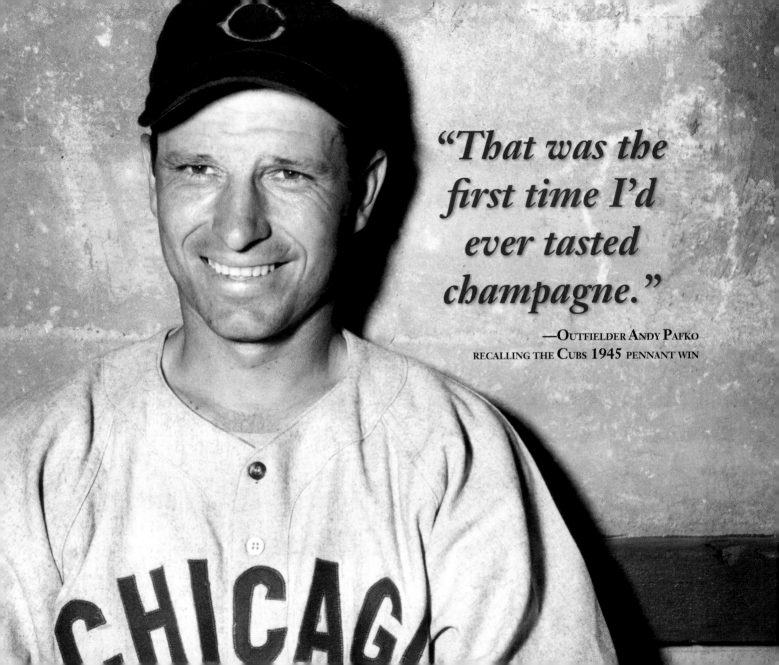

"That was the first time I'd ever tasted champagne."

—Outfielder Andy Pafko
recalling the Cubs 1945 pennant win

CUBS QUIZ

1. Who was the main third baseman in the Tinker to Evers to Chance infield?

. . . .

2. What is the Cubs' single-game record for strikeouts by a left-handed pitcher, and who holds it? (Hint: He's pictured below.)

3. Who is the last pitcher to win 20 games for the Cubs?

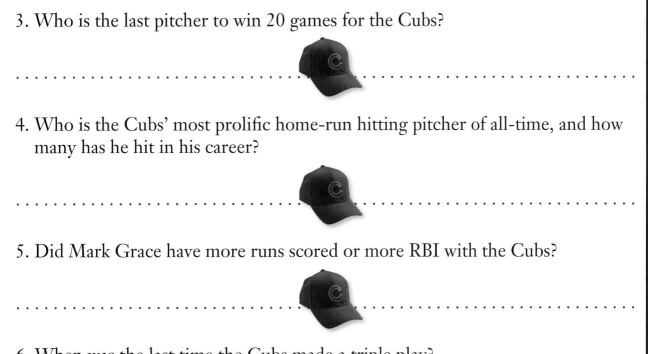

. . . .

4. Who is the Cubs' most prolific home-run hitting pitcher of all-time, and how many has he hit in his career?

. . . .

5. Did Mark Grace have more runs scored or more RBI with the Cubs?

. . . .

6. When was the last time the Cubs made a triple play?

CHAPTER TWO

"MEN IN BLUE"

"Here's to you, Men in Blue,

You're the cream of the crop.

You're a team built on dreams,

You'll go right to the top.

And sure as there's ivy on the center field wall,

The Men in Blue are gonna win it all."

—JAMES RITZ AND ALLEN PETROWSKI
(SUNG BY JODY DAVIS, LEON DURHAM, KEITH MORELAND, RICK SUTCLIFFE, AND GARY WOODS, 1984)

The '84 Cubs celebrate after clinching their division. From left to right: Ron Cey, Larry Bowa, Rick Sutcliffe, Jody Davis, and Leon Durham.

"And when I saw the Cubs and I saw Wrigley Field, right there and then it was something special . . . there was just something I loved about that ballpark."

—RON SANTO, ON HOW HIS YOUTHFUL TV IMPRESSIONS INFLUENCED HIS DECISION TO SIGN WITH THE CUBS

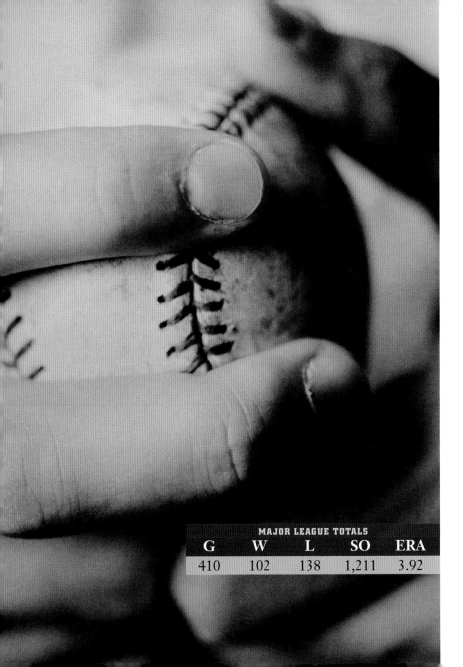

MAJOR LEAGUE TOTALS				
G	W	L	SO	ERA
410	102	138	1,211	3.92

WELCOME TO CHICAGO!

On May 13, 1960, pitcher Don Cardwell joined the Cubs in a trade, coming over from the Philadelphia Phillies with Ed Bouchee for Tony Taylor and Cal Neeman. Two days later, during his first start for the Cubs, Cardwell pitched a no-hitter in the second game of a doubleheader against the St. Louis Cardinals. A walk in the first inning was the only blemish, and he retired the last 26 batters he faced.

TINKER TO EVERS TO CHANCE

They were the glue that held the Cubs together back in 1906, '07, and '08—the slick double-play combo of shortstop Joe Tinker, second baseman Johnny Evers, and first baseman Frank Chance. The legendary trio anchored the infield in the early 1900s, bringing flash and dash to a team that was at the top of its game—**they were three team leaders with a knack for making the big play.**

The first double play recorded by the trio came in 1902—the day after they first appeared together in the infield. Chance had been the team's backup catcher when Cubs manager Frank Selee moved him to first base. Third baseman Joe Tinker was shifted to short, replacing Evers, who filled in for second baseman Bobby Lowe. When Lowe broke his ankle on September 2, Evers stepped in as the permanent pivot man. And just like that, **the most famous double-play combination** in history was born.

For all their renown, the stats of Tinker, Evers, and Chance don't match up well with future greats. Double plays

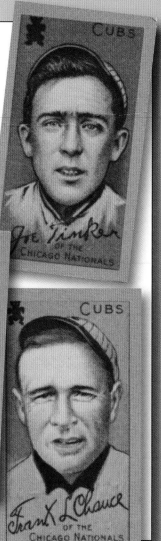

were much less common in the dead-ball era than they are in the modern game, on-base percentages were much lower, and **most hitters who reached base attempted to steal,** eliminating many double-play situations. None of the famed three ranks in baseball's top ten for double plays in a season, and none even ranks at the top of the fielding percentage lists in Cubs annals.

Nevertheless, the trio revolutionized how the positions were played. They crafted new strategies to protect against bunts, steals, and the hit-and-run. Together, they led the Cubs to the World Series four times. And all three went on to manage the club later in their careers.

Franklin P. Adams, a Chicago native and a well-known scribe of the day, penned some of the most famous words ever written about baseball in "Baseball's Sad Lexicon," a poem published in the *New York Evening Mail* on July 10, 1910. In part, he wrote:

These are the saddest of possible words:

"Tinker to Evers to Chance."

Trio of bear cubs, and fleeter than birds:

Tinker and Evers and Chance.

The year "Baseball's Sad Lexicon" was published was the last year the trio took the field together.

While there were certainly far more than three standout performers on the terrific Cubs teams of the early 1900s, thanks to Franklin P. Adams, this trio of bear cubs always got top billing—right up through their Hall of Fame induction (together, of course) in 1946.

A CITY DIVIDED
THE CROSSTOWN RIVALRY

North Side or South Side? It's a distinction Chicagoans cling to with fierce pride. There are some who claim they can cheer for both Chicago teams, but they are certainly the exception, looked upon with skepticism and suspicion by die-harders in Cubbie blue or White Sox black.

The century-old crosstown rivalry began in 1903, when the upstart American League White Sox were only three years old. As a sign of détente between the established National League team and the new league, an intra-city exhibition event called "The City Series" was initiated, and the two teams met on the field for the first time in a 15-game challenge. No records were at stake and nothing affected the outcome of the season. But neither team walked away with bragging rights, either. The series ended with seven wins apiece when one game was rained out, and the

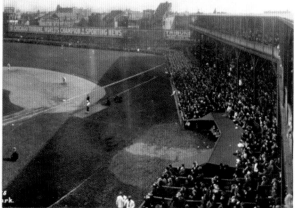

event became a regular staple on the Chicago baseball calendar for the next 40 years.

Eventually, this series morphed into an annual single-game charity exhibition: the Crosstown Classic, or Crosstown Showdown. A popular draw for Chicago fans who piled into stands with cheers and jeers and typical rivalry mischief, this matchup still meant nothing in the standings; however, fans of the victors reveled in a year of bragging rights.

The introduction of interleague play in 1997 ramped up the rivalry. For the first time, these intra-city matchups actually mattered for something other than pride. Through 2008, the teams were dead-even in interleague play, with 33 wins and 33 losses apiece—and there have been six series sweeps that have fanned the flames of the rivalry: four by the Cubs (1998, 2004, 2007, 2008), and two by the Sox (1999, 2008). A benches-clearing brawl between the two teams in 2006 only fueled the fire.

Only once have the two Chicago teams met in the postseason: In 1906, the South Side "Hitless Wonders" triumphed over the heavily favored Cubs, taking the world championship in six games.

A. J. Pierzynski plows into Cubs catcher Michael Barrett on May 20, 2006, sparking a benches-clearing brawl moments later.

In 2008, when both teams held first place in their respective divisions, the rivalry was hotter than ever. And as they have been for more than a century, Chicago fans remain divided by fervent pride and passion for their team.

FAMOUS FLICKS
FEATURING THE CUBS OR WRIGLEY FIELD

- *Ferris Bueller's Day Off*
- ***A League of Their Own***
- ***The Babe***
- *This Old Cub*
- **Rookie of the Year**
- *Forever Loyal: A Salute to the Cubs Fans and Their Field*
- *Chasing October: A Fan's Crusade*
- ***The Blues Brothers***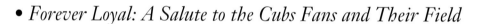
- *Wrigley Field: Beyond the Ivy*

YOSH KAWANO

There is a popular saying in American business about a longtime employee: "He knows where the bodies are buried." Yosh Kawano is that person in the Chicago Cubs organization.

Kawano, who was born in 1921, first went to work for the Cubs as a clubhouse attendant in 1943 and served as the team's equipment manager or assistant from the 1953 season until the start of the 2008 season, when he retired just shy of his 87th birthday.

Initially, to make an impression on the Cubs, Kawano stowed away on a boat from the California mainland to reach Catalina Island, the spring training home of the team at the time.

When the team was sold from the Wrigley family to the Tribune Company in 1981, a clause was inserted in the deal guaranteeing Kawano a job for life.

A man who could probably tell a million clubhouse stories, but who has kept his lip zipped in the interest of discretion, Kawano could always be identified in the Cubs dugout by his trademark white floppy hat and khaki pants. When Yosh Kawano Day was celebrated at Wrigley Field on June 26, 2008, the Cubs' most loyal employee threw out a ceremonial first pitch and led the singing of "Take Me Out to the Ball Game" during the seventh-inning stretch.

"Who says there's no loyalty in baseball?... Wow!"

—CUBS HALL OF FAMER RYNE SANDBERG DISCUSSING YOSH KAWANO

GREG MADDUX
THE ONE THAT GOT AWAY—TWICE

Oh, what could have been—what *should* have been.

As the 2008 baseball season came to a close, 42-year-old right-hander Greg Maddux had 355 wins under his belt. Widely recognized as one of the top pitchers in major-league history, Maddux was on his way to sure Hall of Fame enshrinement.

With a nickname like "Mad Dog," one might expect an intimidating, fearsome presence. Yet Maddux is perhaps the most unprepossessing superstar in baseball. He is listed at 6′0″ and 195 pounds—and none too toned at that—and his fastball has the giddy-up of a Volkswagen, clocking in at around 85 miles per hour. Yet, during his storied career, Maddux has racked up more than 3,300 strikeouts. He is perhaps the smartest pitcher

of all time—a crafty thrower who hits the corners and fools batters more than overpowering them.

Drafted by the Cubs in 1984, Maddux worked his way through the minors before arriving in Chicago in late '86. He got off to a shaky start in 1987—officially his rookie year—stumbling through a 6–14 season. But by 1988, when he went 18–8, it was clear that he could be the Cubs' ace for years to come.

This viewpoint was solidified in 1992 when Maddux won 20 games and recorded a 2.18 ERA, a showing that earned him the Cy Young Award as the best pitcher in the National League.

Anyone—everyone—could see that Maddux should be locked up with a long-term contract for whatever he wanted. (Give him the ivy!) Maddux wanted to stay in Chicago.

But they couldn't reach a deal, and as a free agent, Maddux went to the Atlanta Braves to become a living legend, winning a World Series and a multitude of divisional titles, while the Cubs sank to the netherworld of the National League.

With the Braves, Maddux took home three more Cy Young trophies before becoming a free agent again and re-signing with the Cubs in 2004. Fans welcomed him back with open arms.

Maddux won 16 games in 2004 and 13 in 2005, but in the midst of a disappointing 2006 season (the Cubs lost 96 games), Maddux was shipped off to the Los Angeles Dodgers as Cubs fans watched in disbelief. He later signed with San Diego, where, in 2008, he began his 23rd season, earning a spot in the starting rotation at age 42. When Maddux faced the Cubs at Wrigley Field in May 2008, he received a standing ovation.

Although it doesn't count as a terrible trade, there's no doubt that the original loss of Maddux in free agency ranks near the top of the Cubs' all-time personnel mistakes. Even as he nears the end of his career, Cubs fans will always agree that Maddux looks best in Cubbie blue.

	MAJOR LEAGUE TOTALS				
G	W	L	WP	SO	ERA
744	355	227	.610	3,371	3.16

MAJOR LEAGUE TOTALS				
G	W	L	WP	ERA
106	42	29	.592	3.51

WHAT MIGHT HAVE BEEN

Right-hander **Mark Prior** might be the human incarnation of the Billy Goat Curse. Such talent. Such promise. Such a disaster. The 6'5", 225-pound pitcher was a No. 1 draft pick who rocketed through the Cubs farm system and won 18 big-league games in 2003.

Several of Prior's many stays on the disabled list for arm injuries followed his unraveling on the mound during the infamous playoff game on October 14, 2003, when fan Steve Bartman's attempt to catch a foul ball seemed to jinx the Cubs' attempt to reach the World Series. Wrapped around six minor-league rehab stints, Prior was 6–4 for the Cubs in 2004 and 11–7 in 2005. Although damage from the Bartman incident was more mental than physical, Prior was never the same pitcher for the Cubs. In 2006, he had a 1–6 record and threw only 43⅔ innings. Then, he missed the entire 2007 season due to injury. When Prior's contract was up after the '07 season, he signed with the San Diego Padres as a free agent but, again, missed the entire 2008 season due to injury.

RICK MONDAY: AMERICAN HERO

Rick Monday, already a fan favorite for the way he stalked center field like a lion searching for prey, became an **American hero overnight for a catch completely different from his routine grabs of fly balls.**

On April 25, 1976—the year of the U.S. bicentennial—Monday was patrolling center for the Cubs in a game against the Dodgers in Chavez Ravine. During the fourth inning, two men jumped over an outfield wall, but rather than race across the field waving, typical of such interlopers, they bent to a mysterious task in the field. It took a few moments for Monday to realize what they were up to, but when he recognized that the **men were attempting to burn an American flag,** he dashed toward them, scooped up the flag that was already covered in lighter fluid, and liberated it.

When fans understood what had occurred, they gave Monday a thunderous ovation and he immediately became the toast of the land for his actions. For nearly three decades, Monday proudly displayed the flag in his home, but he now keeps it in a safe-deposit box.

"This flag is doused with lighter fluid. You could smell it. You could feel it on my hand. It was soaking wet."

—RICK MONDAY ON WHAT WAS GOING THROUGH HIS MIND WHEN HE GRABBED THE AMERICAN FLAG FROM PROTESTERS TRYING TO SET IT AFLAME

Tinker...

Born: 1880   Died: 1948

Joe Tinker, the Cubs' everyday shortstop for 11 years, led NL shortstops in fielding four times, in total chances three times, twice each

in putouts and assists, and once in double plays. With great speed, he averaged 28 stolen bases per season for Chicago, once stealing home twice in the same game (tied for the major-league record). He was also as focused on his salary as he was on his game, jumping from team to team after his time with the Cubs—and even to the Federal League—to bump up his pay.

At the height of Tinker's considerable fame, he was also a prominent vaudeville player.

...to Evers...

Born: 1881   Died: 1947

Johnny Evers, a slightly built man who reportedly didn't even weigh 100 pounds as a rookie, was of fiery temperament and scrappy spirit. The second baseman batted .350 in both the '07 and '08 World Series, driving in the winning run to bring home the '08 championship. He never got along well with Tinker—in fact, they developed a feud during their playing days and went decades without speaking to

each other. They only reconciled when they broadcasted the 1938 World Series for the Cubs.

It was Evers who pointed out Fred Merkle's baserunning error in the 1908 pennant race, costing the Giants the pennant.

. . . to Chance

Born: 1877   Died: 1924

First baseman Frank Chance, known as "The Peerless Leader," was the rock of the Cubs franchise, serving as player-manager beginning

in 1905. He was a fan favorite, respected by all in the league for his great play and aggressive style. He compiled a .300 average in 20 World Series games and racked up a lifetime batting average of .296. His .664 winning percentage as a manager (768–389) is the best in Cubs history.

The 116 games the Cubs won in '06 under Chance's leadership remain a major-league record (tied by the Seattle Mariners in 2001).

Who's Harry Steinfeldt?

If ever a man had the right to hate a poem, Harry Steinfeldt was the man. In addition to likely helping its three protagonists into the Hall of Fame, "Baseball's Sad Lexicon" also doomed to anonymity the excellent third baseman who toiled alongside them.

Steinfeldt hit .327 with a league-leading 83 RBI and 176 hits for the 1906 pennant-winning Cubs. A starter on four World Series teams, he batted .471 in Chicago's win over Detroit in the 1907 fall classic. He was also a stellar fielder and basestealer. Nevertheless, he was left out of the poem that immortalized his teammates and was left out of the Hall of Fame as well.

BROKENHEARTED: THE '69 CUBS

It was a season of glory and heartbreak, of soaring hopes and dashed dreams, of wonderful memories and poisonous flashbacks.

Only Chicago baseball fans remember 1969 as the almost-year of the Cubs. All other baseball followers remember the season as the culmination of the worst-to-first, decade-long transformation of the New York Mets. How did those miracles get confused? It was like the unfortunate switching of two babies in a hospital's maternity ward.

Ron Santo, Don Kessinger, Glenn Beckert, and Ernie Banks

When Leo Durocher was hired as manager in 1966, he famously stated, "I'm not the manager of an eighth-place team." He was right—the Cubs finished an embarrassing tenth place that year. But from worse-than-he-thought in '66 to better-than-expected in '69, the Cubs made the turnaround that the Wrigley faithful had hoped for.

As usual, the optimistic Ernie Banks made one of his rhyming predictions: "The Cubs are gonna shine in '69," he said jovially, and, for most of the season, they did. Flanked by a fearsome lineup that included Banks at first, Glenn Beckert at second, Don Kessinger at short, Ron Santo at third, Billy Williams in left field, and Randy Hundley behind the plate, plus Fergie Jenkins and Ken Holtzman as the leaders of the pitching rotation, the Cubs posted a record of 92–70 and stayed in first place from Opening Day until September 10—155 straight days occupying the penthouse of the National League East.

The Cubs won the season opener 7–6 over the Phillies, sparked by Banks's three-run homer in the first, his two-run blast in the third, and Willie Smith's two-run shot in the bottom of the 11th to win the ball game. The next day Williams hit four straight doubles to tie a major-league record, and the Cubs were off to a 16–7 April.

Roughly a million more fans attended games at Wrigley in 1969 than in 1966. And at the end of a 1–0 triumph over the Mets in mid-July, Ron Santo gleefully leaped into the air and clicked his heels together as he ran down the third-base line. It was a spontaneous acrobatic move, and the fans ate it up, so at Durocher's urging, Santo began performing the trick after each Cubs home win.

The entire Cubs infield was selected to the All-Star Game, and, less than a month later, Holtzman pitched the first of his two career no-hitters. Rarely did Cubs fans have it so good. And then it all began to unravel.

It has been suggested that playing a full slate of day games in the summer's heat and humidity, while other teams played at night, took a toll on the Cubs, especially because Durocher didn't use his bench much. The higher the temperature rose, the colder the Cubs got.

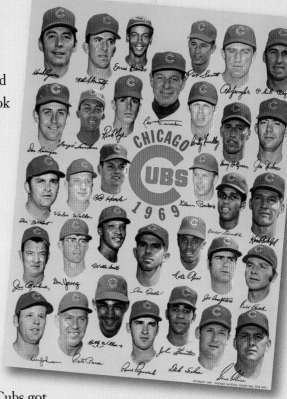

The Mets passed the Cubs like a speeding train on September 10 and clinched the division two weeks later. Just like that, the dream of the Cubs' first World Series appearance in 24 years came to a screeching halt. Cubs fans are still scarred by the crushing end to a fun-filled season.

CUBS CARE

For more than a century, Cubs fans have devoted themselves to the team, rejoicing in the wins, while mourning the losses; following the pickups and acquisitions with a watchful eye; celebrating or bemoaning the trades. Through good times and bad, Cubs fans have proven that they care.

Since 1981, Cubs Care (which teamed with the McCormick Tribune Foundation in 1991) has focused on improving lives in the city of Chicago. Children with special needs, victims of domestic violence, and youth sports programs are among those who have benefited from the fund. The organization also focuses on people living in the neighborhoods around Wrigley Field, providing grants to social service agencies and charitable causes in the immediate vicinity. Since 1991, Cubs Care has granted more than $13 million to Chicago charities.

The team raises money by opening their doors to Cubs fans so that they will open their arms to the community. Fund-raisers include an annual dinner party for fans and players, a 5K run, tours of Wrigley Field, the annual Cubs Convention, and more. In 2005, the players' wives illustrated a children's book entitled *Wrigley Field from A to Z*, donating proceeds to the cause.

While "next year" may always be the time for Cubs fans to celebrate in Wrigleyville, in the meantime, the foundation makes sure the needy have cause to celebrate even when the W flag is not waving from the Wrigley Field scoreboard.

To donate to Cubs Care, visit the Cubs' Web site at www.chicago.cubs.mlb.com. The McCormick Tribune Foundation matches all funds raised—yet another reason for Cubs fans to celebrate.

"You're in a great ballpark
in a great city."

—BILLY WILLIAMS ON THE PRIVILEGE OF PLAYING FOR THE CUBS

MARK "AMAZING" GRACE

Grace is right. The three-time All-Star proved aptly named, manning first base for the Cubs gracefully from 1988 through 2000 and earning **four Gold Gloves** along the way. Mark Grace was known for being outspoken, direct, and witty, as well as productive on the field.

How productive? Grace topped .300 nine times in his 13-year tenure in Chicago, reaching base frequently (with an excellent .383 on-base percentage) and driving in runs (topping 90 three times, yet never managing to hit the 100 mark). What Grace could *not* do well enough to please critics was hit home runs. He racked up 15 or so each year, topping out with a career high of 17 in 1998. That part of his performance was the only flaw in his game com-

In September 2002, the D-Backs brought Grace in as a relief pitcher in the ninth inning of a 19–1 rout by the Dodgers. After getting the first two batters to fly out, Grace gave up a home run to Dave Ross. He finished the game—and his pitching career—with a 9.00 ERA. His "fastball" clocked in at 65 miles per hour.

pared to traditional first basemen, and "Amazing Grace" was still a very popular Cub.

Grace had the good timing to become a key member of the Cubs when the club took a serious run at the NL pennant in 1989. It was his second season installed at the first sack, and he batted an impressive .314 as the Cubs topped the NL East with a 93–69 record before dropping the National League Championship Series to the San Francisco Giants in five games. However, it wasn't for lack of support from Grace—Mr. Clutch recorded an unbelievable .647 batting average in the series.

Midway through the '89 season, Grace's spirit became much-admired after an on-field incident with Frank DiPino, who was pitching for the rival St. Louis Cardinals. Enraged by a brushback pitch from DiPino, Grace charged the mound and inflamed a bench-clearing brawl. Without a doubt, a player could always score points with Cubs backers by standing up to the Cards.

Grace is **one of nearly 300 major-leaguers who have hit for the cycle,** cracking a single, a double, a triple, and a home run in one game. His went into the books on May 9, 1993, in a game against San Diego. Typical of the team at the time, however, the Cubs lost the game 5–4.

Despite the passionate protests of Cubs fans, Grace, who led all major-leaguers in total hits and doubles during the '90s, left at the end of the

2000 season when the Cubs did not renew his contract. He signed with the Arizona Diamondbacks, where he quickly brought home a World Series ring in 2001 during the twilight of his playing days.

MAJOR LEAGUE TOTALS			
G	HR	RBI	BA
2,245	173	1,146	.303

ON TOP OF THE WORLD

For many years, ballparks of the modern era were constructed on acres of land that used to grow corn or soybeans and could accommodate thousands of automobiles. But part of the charm of Wrigley Field has been its urban location, tucked into a mostly residential neighborhood.

For decades, crafty fans in the apartment buildings across the street from the Friendly Confines perched themselves on the rooftops or in front of the windows of the higher floors to catch the on-field action for free. Then in the late 1980s, when the Cubs began filling the park regularly, the demand for rooftop seating really took off.

Initially, watching a Cubs game from a rooftop was all rather innocent. People who lived in the buildings might wander up to

the roof to catch a couple of innings. They might even invite friends over to watch a game.

But then, the idea of watching a game from a rooftop became a cool and trendy thing to do, and with no admission charged, it was a steal. Ultimately, however, building owners realized they could offer renters something more than pristine hardwood floors and air-conditioning—something on the order of Cubs season tickets. Bleachers began sprouting up on the roofs of several buildings in the late '80s and admission was charged. No other major-league stadium has this type of seating.

Like most novel ideas, rooftop operations eventually evolved into a business. Today, a company named "Wrigleyville Rooftops" sells tickets for three apartment buildings. Food, beverages, and parking are included at a cost of $90–200 per person, depending on the date and game. In case of poor weather, the game can also be viewed from a third-floor "air-conditioned sky box."

Not to be left out of the party, in 1998—recognizing that the rooftops were more than just a place where people could work on their suntan, grill up some burgers, or grow flowers—the city of Chicago began requiring building owners to purchase a special license and pay an amusement tax. With this license, operators are allowed to sell beer and wine on game days.

In one way or another, everyone seemed to be benefiting from rooftop watching—except for the team. The Cubs did not share in the profits from rooftop ticket sales, so in the 2000s, the team got ornery about the status quo. In 2003, claiming that the rooftops were a $10 million business, the team began hinting that it might try to put up unattractive screens or build higher outfield walls to block free access to their product. Team owners eventually secured a deal giving them a 17 percent share of rooftop revenue. Now the Cubs get a chunk of the proceeds, the building owners protect their investment, and fans that prefer rooftops over bleachers still get to watch baseball games live and in person. The unique tradition continues.

Geovany Soto, Carlos Marmol, Kerry Wood, Carlos Zambrano, Aramis Ramirez, Alfonso Soriano, and Kosuke Fukudome show off their National League All-Star jerseys. (Not pictured: Ryan Dempster)

EIGHT IS ENOUGH...FOR A RECORD

When a blister kept Kerry Wood from pitching in the 2008 All-Star Game, he was replaced by teammate Carlos Marmol, allowing the Cubs to tie a National League record with eight players—including two rookie starters—on the roster.

The 1943 Cardinals, 1956 Reds, and 1960 Pirates also sent eight players to the All-Star Game. The major-league record of nine players from one team was set by the 1958 Yankees.

Here's a look at the record-tying contingent that represented the Cubbies at the final All-Star Game ever played at Yankee Stadium—"The House that Ruth Built."

OF Kosuke Fukudome—A veteran of nine seasons in Japan, Fukudome's first year in the majors saw him leading all rookies in several hitting categories at the time of his selection to the All-Star Game's starting nine. During the second of Kosuke's two at-bats, FOX displayed his name and statistics in Japanese characters.

C Geovany Soto—The first rookie catcher ever to start an All-Star Game for the NL, Soto brought a .288 batting average to the mid-summer classic and was later named the 2008 NL Rookie of the Year. (In 1990, rookie catcher Sandy Alomar, Jr., started the All-Star Game for the AL.)

P Ryan Dempster—Although he was elected to the All-Star team for his first-rate numbers as a starter, Dempster revisited his former job as closer by coming into the game in the ninth inning and striking out the side in order, forcing extra frames.

P Kerry Wood—The opposition was batting less than .200 against Wood through the first half of the season, which allowed him to make his second trip to the midsummer classic. Unfortunately, a blister on his pitching hand forced him to sit out the game.

Cubs manager Lou Piniella was also a member of the 2008 All-Star Team—as part of the coaching staff.

P Carlos Marmol—The Cubs' set-up man, who posted a sub-2.00 ERA through May, was the relief pitcher with the next highest vote total, so he was added to the roster in place of Wood. He retired the AL in order in the 13th.

3B Aramis Ramirez—Ramirez made his second career All-Star Game appearance after a first half in which he hit .298 with men in scoring position. He drew a walk in his only at bat.

OF Alfonso Soriano—Though injured and unable to play, Soriano wanted to say farewell to Yankee Stadium, the park where the seven-time All-Star began his major-league career in 1999.

P Carlos Zambrano—At the end of May 2008, Zambrano was off to his best start at 7–1 with a 2.44 ERA. He pitched two score-less innings in his third All-Star Game and drew laughs with a playful, high-arcing pitch over the head of Manny Ramirez.

JOE PEPITONE: A LITTLE BIT OF PEP

When the writers of the popular 1990s sitcom *Seinfeld* had hipster doofus character Cosmo Kramer triggering a dugout-clearing brawl at a fantasy baseball camp, it was none other than Joe Pepitone they had him beaning with a pitch. Those who followed Pepitone's free-spirited career might call such screenwriting "art imitating life."

Pepitone spent his first eight seasons with the Yankees but served the Cubs from 1970 to '73. While in the Bronx, he was a three-time All-Star and three-time Gold Glove winner at first base.

Pepitone held a unique appeal to fans, including those who purchased a 1975 edition of *Foxy Lady* magazine in which he posed not in his uniform, but in his birthday suit. While with the Cubs, Pepitone could be heard bellowing out "Take Me Out to the Ball Game" in the seventh-inning stretch at Wrigley Field long before Harry Caray made it popular. The charismatic first baseman and sometimes outfielder, who batted a career-high .307 in 1971, was known for living life full-throttle and even for lighting teammates' shoes on fire.

It's said that as a rookie with the Yankees in 1962, Pepitone spent his entire $25,000 signing bonus on the way to spring training in Florida, arriving in a shiny new Ford Thunderbird, pulling a brand new boat, and accompanied by a newly purchased dog.

Pepitone has been a regular on the fantasy camp circuit, and although he's never charged the mound to fight a sitcom character, one fantasy camper pointed out: "Joe Pepitone is as nutty as they say, but he really knows his baseball."

> The longest hitting streak of Pepitone's career—19 games—took place while he was with the Cubs in 1971.

LENNIE MERULLO'S JITTERS

Lennie Merullo is one of the last surviving members of the 1945 National League pennant-winning Chicago Cubs. He played seven seasons at shortstop for the North Siders, from 1941 to 1947.

On September 13, 1942, when Merullo's wife was about to give birth to their son, Lennie insisted on staying in the Cubs starting lineup rather than going to the hospital to pace in the waiting room. However, he was a nervous wreck and tied a major-league record by making four errors in one inning. Fortunately, his wife's performance went more smoothly.

The story followed Merullo, and his son was even nicknamed "Boots," not because he was partial to the footwear, but because his dad had booted so many grounders on the day he was born. When his playing days were over, Merullo continued his service with the Cubs, working as a scout. After watching a Negro League game at Comiskey Park, it was Merullo who recommended that the team sign a young African American shortstop named Ernie Banks.

1984: THE DREAM SEASON
TURNS INTO A NIGHTMARE

As far as the Cubs were concerned, George Orwell was right. In the end, 1984 was a nightmare.

After 39 years without a pennant—or any kind of playoff appearance—Cubs fans were as thirsty as desert wanderers deprived of water. During the regular season, the '84 Cubbies did not disappoint. They delighted their faithful followers, posting a 96–65 record and finishing above .500 for the first time since 1972.

When the "Men in Blue" clinched their division on September 24, it was a team effort, but there were some stellar individual performances as well. Future Hall of Famer **Ryne Sandberg** was just starting to come into his own, batting .314 and earning **MVP honors** and his second of nine straight Gold Gloves at second base. Pitcher Rick Sutcliffe, who was acquired in a trade on June 13, was unstoppable,

racking up a 16–1 record for the remainder of the season and garnering a Cy Young Award. And Gary Matthews was a spark plug at the plate, where he recorded a .410 on-base percentage, and in the dugout, where "Sarge" served as a spiritual leader to fan favorites such as Jody Davis, Bobby Dernier, Leon "Bull" Durham, Keith Moreland, Ron Cey, Scott Sanderson, Dennis Eckersley, and others.

From the first pitch of the regular season to the last, it was a dream summer for the Cubbies and their fans. The team cracked the two million mark in attendance for the first time and broke the club's previous record by 500,000. After the final home game, manager Jim Frey walked the team around the field as a "thank you" to the fans. The World Series and destiny beckoned… or so it seemed.

On October 2, the National League Championship Series kicked off at Wrigley Field—the first time the Friendly Confines had seen postseason play in nearly four decades. The Cubs promptly bashed the San Diego Padres 13–0, with five home runs, including one by ace hurler Sutcliffe.

A day later, the Cubs bested the Padres 4–2, as Steve Trout pitched masterfully and stud reliever Lee Smith closed it out. The North Siders led the best-of-five series 2–0 and were one win away from reaching the World Series. But then the unthinkable happened, and, in the blink of an eye, the joyride was over.

Rational Cubs fans knew not to be overconfident. Although the Cubs had the best record in the NL, the remaining three games would be played in San Diego—a nice place to visit if you want to surf or go to the zoo, but not where the Cubs wanted to duke it out for a trip to the Series.

Cynical Cubs fans will tell you that they saw it coming all along. As the NLCS moved west, syndicated political columnist and baseball writer George Will predicted that the Padres would sweep the last three games.

It was a self-fulfilling prophecy for the Cubs, who promptly lost to the Padres 7–1, 7–5, and 6–3. The final game was the most heart-wrenching. With **star hurler Sutcliffe** on the mound, Chicago led 3–0 going into the bottom of the sixth. But San Diego scored two, then tied it in the seventh when an innocent ground ball dribbled through first  baseman Leon Durham's legs. With the Cubs and their ace unraveling, the Padres took the lead for good on a Tony Gwynn double. Most Cubs fans have still not recovered from the heartbreak…and they probably never will.

"There's nothing with this team that more pitching, more fielding, and more hitting couldn't help."

—Cubs first baseman Bill Buckner during 1981 when a labor strike interrupted the season and the Cubs finished 38–65—the worst record in the National League East

MR. BEHIND-THE-SCENES
ARNE HARRIS

No matter how poorly the Cubs played for most of his tenure at WGN, Arne Harris could be counted on to find the silver lining in a dark cloud, usually in the form of pretty women cheering from the Wrigley Field seats. Fans of the North Siders—at least male ones—were grateful.

Harris never hit a baseball for the Cubs, rarely made an appearance in front of the camera, and never overshadowed the likes of announcers Jack Brickhouse or Harry Caray. Still, Cubs fans knew his name—perhaps more than followers of any other team have ever identified with a TV producer and director.

Harris joined his hometown Chicago station while attending Drake University in Iowa in 1956. He also served a three-year stint as public-address announcer for the Harlem Globetrotters. However, it was his work from the WGN truck outside Wrigley Field for 38 years that endeared Harris to Cubs fans and had popular announcers like Brickhouse, Caray, and Steve Stone praising his efforts during almost every broadcast.

Under Harris's direction, Cubs games were entertainment events as much as sporting contests. The right cameras were called on at the right time. And if the sun was shining in the stands, that frequently meant air time for the beautiful women in their Cubs caps and halter tops.

Chicago Tribune columnist Bob Verdi once wrote that Arne Harris was closing in on Jack Brickhouse's record for "most Chicago baseball losses watched, one man, lifetime."

In 2001, Harris was dining with his wife and Cubs announcer Chip Caray when a heart ailment took his life at age 67. The Cubs placed a flag in his honor on the roof of Wrigley Field, as if looking down on all those lovely patrons.

ALMOST PERFECT

On September 9, 1965, **Bob Hendley pitched the greatest game of his major-league career for the Cubs—** and lost. He threw a one-hitter and surrendered only one unearned run to the Dodgers. Unfortunately, Hendley's shining moment was overshadowed by the fact that **Dodger southpaw Sandy Koufax tossed a perfect game.**

In the 1–0 victory, Koufax was magnificent. Although he was close to retirement due to recurring elbow problems, the legendary Dodger hurler struck out 14 batters while facing the minimum 27 hitters.

On the other side of the coin, Hendley spent seven years in the majors—parts of three seasons with the Cubs—and finished with a 48–52 lifetime record. Although he did rack up double-digit win totals with other clubs, the most Hendley won in a season for Chicago was four. **The showdown against Koufax was the pinnacle of Hendley's career,** and to Cubs doomsayers it figured that a guy could pitch so terrifically and still lose.

"Why not us?"

—Dusty Baker
ON HIS TEAM BREAKING
THE CURSE

MUST READS
FOR DIE-HARD CUBS FANS

Holy Cow! by Harry Caray and Bob Verdi

Wrigleyville by Peter Golenbock

Cubs: Where Have You Gone? by Fred Mitchell

Mr. Cub by Ernie Banks and Jim Enright

The Game Is Easy, Life Is Hard: The Story of Ferguson Jenkins, Jr. by Dorothy Turcotte

Out at Home by Milt Pappas, Wayne Mausser, and Larry Names

Cubs Nation by Gene Wojciechowski

Second to Home by Ryne Sandberg and Barry Rozner

Ron Santo: For Love of Ivy by Ron Santo and Randy Minkoff

Where's Harry? by Steve Stone and Barry Rozner

Bleachers: A Summer in Wrigley Field by Lonnie Wheeler

Cubs Journal: Year by Year & Day by Day with the Chicago Cubs Since 1876 by John Snyder

Billy Williams: My Sweet-Swinging Lifetime with the Cubs by Billy Williams and Fred Mitchell

Cubs Forever: Memories from the Men Who Lived Them by Bob Vorwald and Stephen Green

"How blessed I was to be a baseball player and to have played for the Cubs in the city of Chicago, with the greatest fans in the world. Cubs fans are like no other fans. . . ."

—ERNIE BANKS, FROM *FEW AND CHOSEN* BY RON SANTO AND PHIL PEPE

THE BLACK CAT INCIDENT

On September 9, 1969, the Cubs had been in first place since Opening Day—154 straight days—though, by that time, they were hanging on by their fingernails. It had been 24 years since the Billy Goat Curse was imposed on the Cubs, and on this particular day, it was as if the disgruntled beast had sent an emissary from the grave.

Emotions were brittle during the two-game series at Shea Stadium. The Mets had been chasing Chicago all season while the Cubs saw their dream slipping away.

And so it was in the top of the first—Billy Williams stood at the plate while Ron Santo waited in the on-deck circle. Suddenly, a black cat appeared on the field and ran a lap around Santo before scurrying into the Cubs dugout. Folks of average superstition believe that black cats are harbingers of bad luck—portents of doom—and the Cubs' stunned third baseman said he was unnerved by the cat. The Mets scored two runs in the bottom of the first and went on to an easy 7–1 victory, cutting the Cubs' lead in the standings to a half game.

The Cubs fell to the Phillies the next day, as well, relinquishing first place to the Mets in the process. Neither the black cat nor the Cubs' hopes for a pennant were seen again that season.

"It's one of the greatest ballclubs ever to put on a uniform that never won the World Series."

—Billy Williams, from *My Sweet-Swinging Lifetime with the Cubs* by Billy Williams and Fred Mitchell

MILT PAPPAS: A DISAPPOINTING NO-NO

Milt Pappas was an excellent pitcher who won 209 games and compiled a 3.40 ERA in a 17-year career that ended with the Cubs in 1973. Son of Greek parents, Pappas had enjoyed several exceptional years with the Baltimore Orioles early in his career before being shipped to the National League and pitching for Cincinnati and Atlanta prior to arriving in Chicago in 1970.

Pappas **pitched one of the greatest games in Cubs history,** but the ending of what should have been a fantasy day was tinged with controversy. Normally, pitching a no-hitter in the major leagues is considered the highlight of a hurler's career. Sure, Pappas's no-no on **September 2, 1972,** was a special achievement, but it was probably the only one that felt like somewhat of a letdown. That's because, if not for home plate umpire Bruce Froemming's controversial call, the Pappas game would have been an even rarer gem—a perfect game.

In 1972, the Cubs were having a fairly successful year and would finish in second place in their division a few weeks later with an 85–70 record. Pappas went to the mound to face the San Diego Padres on that fateful day, and from the start his good stuff crackled. The Padres were unable to reach first base. One after another, they were retired on grounders, strikeouts, or fly balls. Meanwhile, the Cubs built an 8–0 lead. As the game went on, the 11,144 spectators in attendance became more and more excited.

At the time, no Cubs pitcher had ever thrown a perfect game. In the top of the ninth, John Jeter hit a fly ball to left-center. At first it seemed that center fielder Bill North would make the play easily, but when North slipped and fell, **Pappas and everyone in the ballpark collectively felt their heart sink into the pit of their stomach.** Then suddenly, Billy Williams rushed in out of left field, literally, to make a near shoestring catch to save the day—and the perfect game.

The next batter, Fred Kendall, grounded out to short. At that point it was 26 men up, 26 men down. Batter number 27 was Larry Stahl, pinch-hitting for pitcher Al Severinsen.

As he'd been doing all day, Pappas got ahead in the count. He worked the count to 1–2 and needed one strike to complete the perfect game. Froemming called the next two pitches balls, running the count full. The irritated hurler, who jawed at the umpire in Greek, thought the last pitch should have been called strike three. The tension in the ballpark was palpable. The zeros on the scoreboard advertised what was going on. On a full count, Pappas fired, but, once again, his pitch was called a ball. Stahl trotted to first, and the perfect game was erased. Pappas induced Garry Jestadt to pop up to second baseman Carmen Fanzone, ending the game as a no-hitter.

It was clearly a stellar accomplishment—one that most pitchers never reach in their entire career—but perfection was so close, and a once-in-a-lifetime chance had slipped away.

10,000 Ws

No one who was around for the Cubs' 10,000th victory—a 7–6, ten-inning triumph over the Colorado Rockies at Coors Field on April 23, 2008—was around for the team's first one, which was registered in 1876. The win over the Rockies made the Cubs **the second team in major-league history to record 10,000 wins,** behind the New York/San Francisco Giants, who attained the milestone in 2005.

Shortstop Ryan Theriot's single drove in the winning run. "I hope the next 10,000 are easier," he quipped.

Cubs fans celebrate the 10,000th win in franchise history. Victory No. 1 came on April 25, 1876, as the Cubs topped the Louisville Grays 4–0.

Alfonso Soriano, Jim Edmonds, and Kosuke Fukudome share in a celebratory hop as the Cubs outfielders did after each victory in 2008.

"Mitch
pitches like
his hair is
on fire."

—MARK GRACE COMMENTING ON
MITCH "WILD THING" WILLIAMS,
RELIEF PITCHER FOR THE CUBS IN
1989 AND 1990

STEVE STONE: TELLING IT LIKE IT IS

Steve Stone was a solid major-league pitcher during a career that spanned 1971 through 1981 and included a 25–7 season with the Baltimore Orioles that earned him a Cy Young Award in 1980. But even he admits that many fans only know him as a guy who talks into a microphone.

Stone was the longtime partner of Harry Caray, the guy who provided details of the game when Caray omitted them and brought Caray back to Earth if one of his tangents strayed too far from the ballpark. Stone also distinguished himself with straight-shooting commentary on the air after Caray died. But he split with the Cubs in 2004, when it seemed tension with certain team members exceeded the bounds of common sense. After a break, Stone is back in the public eye on the South Side as a color baseball analyst for the White Sox.

Steve Stone and Harry Caray

CUBS QUIZ

1. Which Cubs Hall of Fame player returned to the organization as a minor-league manager in the 2000s?

. . . .

2. What uniform piece did Greg Maddux donate to the Baseball Hall of Fame from his second tour with the Cubs?

. . . .

3. After being a player and a coach for the Cubs, what was **Billy Williams's** most recent title with the team?

4. What manager oversaw the Cubs before gaining bigger fame with the Yankees?

. . . .

5. What piece of equipment did **Mark Bellhorn** contribute to the Baseball Hall of Fame?

. . . .

6. Who was Harry Christopher Carabina and how was he affiliated with the Cubs?

1. Second baseman Ryne Sandberg; 2. The Cubs cap he wore during the April 2005 game he pitched against Roger Clemens and the Houston Astros—the first time since 1892 that 300-game winners faced off in the National League; 3. Special assistant to the president; 4. Joe McCarthy, who led the Cubs to the 1929 pennant; 5. The bat used by the switch-hitter to hit home runs from both sides of the plate in the same inning of a 2002 game; 6. Harry Christopher Carabina is the birth name of beloved broadcaster Harry Caray.

CHAPTER THREE

"GO CUBS GO"

"Go Cubs Go!

Go Cubs Go!

Hey Chicago, whaddaya say,

The Cubs are gonna win today!"

—LYRICS BY STEVE GOODMAN, 1984

A stunned Aramis Ramirez sits alone in the dugout after the Cubs lost to the Marlins in Game 7 of the 2003 NLCS.

"Wait 'til next year."

—Motto of Die-hard Cubs Fans

A PROPHETIC ENCOUNTER

As a youth growing up in Northern California in the 1960s, future Cubs play-by-play man Pat Hughes and his brother managed to sneak into the visiting Cubs locker room before a game against the Giants at Candlestick Park. Pat vividly recalls seeing Cubs greats Billy Williams, Ernie Banks, and Ron Santo, the legendary third baseman, nine-time All-Star, and five-time Gold Glove winner, with whom he would share the broadcast booth some 30 years later.

Ron Santo and Pat Hughes

THE FLAMETHROWIN' CANADIAN

Ferguson Jenkins: tough, fiercely competitive, remarkably consistent—and undoubtedly **one of the greatest pitchers in Cubs history.** During his first stint with the team (1966–1973), Jenkins exhibited the excellence and steadfastness of a true baseball great. No Cub since the dead-ball era of the early 1900s has neared his record for consistency.

Signed by Philadelphia in 1963, the 6'5" right-handed flamethrower found himself wearing Cubbie blue in 1966, after the Cubs all but stole him from the Phillies in what turned out to be a decidedly lopsided trade. Jenkins quickly stepped up and became one of the National League's best.

> During the off-seasons of his first few years in the majors, Jenkins played basketball for the Harlem Globetrotters.

In 1967, his first full year as a starter, Jenkins posted his first 20-win season. And then he just kept winning, racking up more than 20 victories in each of the next five years as well. **His streak of six straight seasons with 20 or more wins is a feat no other pitcher has accomplished since.**

Fergie was a stalwart on the mound, also *completing* at least 20 games in each of those 20-win seasons. When he won the Cy Young Award in 1971, Jenkins threw 30 complete games. Entire rosters of pitchers don't even come close to that these days. And in four of those seasons, he also threw more than 300 innings. Today's leaders in innings pitched might not even crack 230.

Exhibiting pinpoint control and the ability to change speeds at will, the three-time All-Star unleashed a solid fastball and a mean slider. He struck out a career-high 274 with the Cubs in 1970, one of the best marks in team history. In

fact, Fergie was only the seventh player in major-league history to record 3,000 career strikeouts.

And as if that weren't enough, this fierce competitor had another weapon up his sleeve: his prowess at the plate. Given his all-around athletic skill, it's no surprise that Jenkins took pride in his hitting. Most pitchers enjoy clouting big blows, especially since no one expects it of them, but Jenkins relished the task more than most. His offense kept him in the line-up late in close contests and helped him complete nearly half of his 594 career starts.

After Jenkins uncharacteristically went 14–16 in 1973, the team shipped him to the Texas Rangers, where he promptly proved the move was a mistake by leading the league with 25 wins. By the time he finished his career back with the Cubs in 1982 and '83, he ranked among baseball's all-time leaders with 284 wins, 49 shut-outs, and 3,192 strikeouts. In 1991, the Chatham, Ontario, native became **the first Canadian elected to the Baseball Hall of Fame.**

MAJOR LEAGUE TOTALS			
G	HR	RBI	BA
2,017	138	775	.275

THE COLORFUL CARDENAL

Remembered and beloved by fans perhaps as much for his hairdo and colorful excuses as for his solid contributions to the team, Jose Cardenal was an integral player on the Cubs roster from 1972 through 1977.

A reliable line-drive hitter and aggressive baserunner with good speed, the Cuban-born outfielder played for nine teams throughout his 18 seasons in the majors. His six-season stint with the Cubs was his longest stay in any one place. His best year was undoubtedly 1973, when he was voted Chicago Player of the Year after leading the Cubs in hitting (.303), doubles (33), and steals (19).

Cardenal has said he enjoyed entertaining the fans by clowning around in the outfield, not simply by providing base hits. On occasion, he allegedly brought extra baseballs to the outfield with him and juggled them. He also entertained fans, perhaps less intentionally, with the colorful stories and offbeat excuses he gave to Cubs management. Once, he was scratched from the lineup because he claimed his eyes were swollen shut when he woke up that morning. Another time he said he failed to sleep the night before because loud crickets had kept him awake all night.

Excuses or not, Cardenal performed, turning in consistently solid performances for the Cubs until his stats slipped in '77, and he was shipped off to his next team, the Phillies.

On August 2, 1979, the Phillies sold Cardenal to the New York Mets during the first game of a doubleheader between the two teams. He was a member of the Phillies in the first game, which they won. After the swap, he donned a Mets uniform and switched to the New York dugout for the second game, which they won. So even though the two teams split the double-header, Cardenal's team won both games.

RUTH'S CALLED SHOT

Did he or didn't he? That is the unanswerable question. When Babe Ruth swatted his 1932 World Series home run off Charlie Root after wagging his finger at A) the pitcher; B) the umpire; C) the fans, was he signaling that he had one strike left in his at-bat or was he really pointing to the outfield and predicting where he would smash a homer?

The scene is one of the most debated moments in baseball history. If it had occurred more recently, it would have been replayed on television over and over again, but given the era, film footage of the moment is extremely rare. Those who believe in the image of a powerful Ruth, who seemed larger than life, cling to the story. It fits in neatly with the myth of Ruth as a superhuman hitter, and he did laugh his way around the bases. Ruth did not immediately play up the incident with sportswriters on the scene, and only one wrote the story the way it was later passed down.

As time went on, though, Ruth pretty much adopted the tale—with a wink. For his part, Root said, "No way!"—if he thought Ruth had humiliated him in that manner, he would have decked him with an inside fastball in retaliation.

1945 SEASON
THE LAST PENNANT

By 1945, Cubs fans felt like the team was in a drought. After all, they'd won the National League pennant like clockwork on the three-year rotation plan in 1929, 1932, 1935, and 1938. So by '45, seven years had passed without a pennant, and fans felt the team was long overdue for a return to the World Series. Little did they know....

The Cubs won 98 games in 1945, finishing first by a three-game margin over the Cardinals. A September 23 victory over the Pirates was propelled by an Andy Pafko grand slam, giving the Cubs a crucial 1½-game lead in the standings before the pennant-clincher came with a 4–3 win over the Pirates on September 29.

This was the last season of baseball disrupted by World War II, and it was not the strongest Cubs team, merely the strongest NL team available. Most of the Cubs' best players had medical deferments, or else they would have been overseas. The Cardinals were missing future Hall of Famers Stan Musial and Enos Slaughter.

Cubs first baseman Phil Cavarretta's .355 batting average led the league. However, the acquisition of an underrated player at the end of July was the key to securing the pennant.

Pitcher Hank Borowy no longer fit in with the Yankees' plans, primarily because cantankerous team president Larry MacPhail didn't like him. The Cubs essentially stole Borowy for $97,000, and he went 11–2 with his new team. Add in the 10 wins Borowy had with New York before the trade, and the hurler had a fine 21-win campaign. That was probably the only time the Yankees, who were always clobbering the Cubs in the World Series, ever did them a favor.

The Cubs also received an unexpectedly solid year from Paul Derringer, a quality pitcher in his time who was approaching the end of his career. At age 39, Derringer finished 16–11 for the North Siders and retired after the 1945 World Series.

But the Detroit Tigers had also worked hard to capture the AL pennant, edging the Washington Senators by 1½ games. Hal Newhouser, the Tigers' ace, finished 25–9 with a 1.81 ERA during this pivotal stretch of his Hall of Fame career.

Borowy, who had been so important during the last two months of the regular season, seemed out of sorts in the Series after his opening-game win. Claude Passeau, the Cubs' steadiest pitcher during the war years, who had recorded a 17–9 mark during the 1945 regular season, pitched a one-hitter in Game 3.

The Cubs pushed the Series to seven games but lost the final game 9–3, marking the seventh straight World Series loss for the franchise. Nobody imagined it would be more than 60 years and counting before the team even *appeared* in another fall classic—not even William Sianis, who was ejected from Wrigley Field with his goat during this Series and infamously placed a curse on the club.

Little did fans realize that the era of a World Series loss every three years would soon come to be appreciated as the "good old days."

(Left to right): *Phil Cavarretta, Hank Borowy, Andy Pafko, and Bill Nicholson*

THE FRIENDLY CONFINES
WARM AND WELCOMING WRIGLEY FIELD

The lights are on, ticket prices have skyrocketed, but Wrigley Field is still the same ballpark where Cubs greats have shined since the days of Cy Williams and Hippo Vaughn. It's where Gabby beat the darkening skies, Lee and Borowy dazzled, Santo clicked his heels, Banks smashed No. 500, Fergie went the distance, Ryno showed his grit, Harry sang, and Sammy surpassed 61. It's home.

Nestled in the Wrigleyville neighborhood on the north side of Chicago is **a beloved architectural wonder** born as Weeghman Park in 1914, renamed Cubs Park in 1920, and known as Wrigley Field since 1926. Built to house Charles Weeghman's upstart Federal League team, the stadium was one of the first of a generation of ballparks constructed of steel and concrete. Original construction cost was $250,000, which wouldn't buy a utility infielder these days.

Over the years, the ballpark has undergone many changes, large and small. But in 1937, the Wrigley Field that present-day fans so adore took shape. In a major remodeling project spearheaded by new owner P. K. Wrigley and executed by 23-year-old Bill Veeck, Jr., new outfield stands and enlarged bleachers were built, boxes and grandstand seats were refashioned to offer fans a better view of the field, and a huge, manually operated scoreboard was erected behind the center-field bleachers. Flags of NL teams were displayed atop the scoreboard in the order of each day's standings, and a brick wall surrounded fair territory.

And then, of course, came the ivy. To give the field a more "woodsy" appearance so that it would be more closely associated with the word *park* than *stadium*, Veeck installed more than 500 ivy plants. Broadcasters and fans took to calling the park "Beautiful Wrigley Field."

Since then, there have been many other smaller scale alterations, but there was one change that was more than 40 years in the making. In 1941, P. K. Wrigley was planning to follow the lead of other clubs and install lights at the park. In fact, the lights had already been delivered to the field and were waiting to be installed. But after the attack on Pearl Harbor, Wrigley decided to donate the steel to the war effort instead. And for the next 47 years, the Cubs played on in Wrigley Field in the light of day, a practice that only added to the charm of the ballpark.

But in 1988, under pressure from Cubs management and Major League Baseball, **the Cubs became the last team in the majors to install lights** for nighttime play. But even today, baseball is still mostly a daytime experience at the Friendly Confines.

Beautiful Wrigley Field, with all its quirks and old-time charm, remains a place that every baseball fan must visit, if only once, for the joy of basking in the sun at the corner of Clark and Addison, at the mercy of the winds blowing in or out from Lake Michigan, surrounded by the cheers and jeers of the Bleacher Bums, the ivy-covered walls, and the familiar if off-key strains of "Take Me Out to the Ball Game," and soaking in the nostalgia of nearly a century of memories of America's favorite pastime.

ROOKIE CROONER

Before the July 21, 1989, game at Wrigley Field against the San Francisco Giants, Cubs **rookie outfielder Dwight Smith** sang the National Anthem. His singing was acceptable, but no one suggested he immediately retire from baseball and start a new career. And it wasn't exactly a good-luck charm as the Cubs lost the game 4–3. An average hitter for the Cubs from 1989 to 1993, Smith might have been better off sticking to the adage of rookies being seen and not heard.

The last time two players from the same team placed first and second in Rookie of the Year balloting was in 1989, when Jerome Walton of the Cubs won the award while his teammate Dwight Smith was runner-up.

"I'll tell you what's helped me my entire life. I look at baseball as a game. It's something where people can go out, enjoy, and have fun...."

—Legendary broadcaster Harry Caray

STILL WAITING,
BUT 2008 WAS QUITE A RIDE

It was a magical season filled with incredible highs. So when it ended all too soon, it hurt even more than in 2007.

Some thought the 2008 Cubs might be a team of destiny. After all, it had been exactly 100 years since the team's last World Series crown, and they did hold the best record in the National League—and in all of baseball—for much of the season.

Others talked of curses and Bartman and billy goats, claiming that despite the Cubs' 97–64 record—their best since 1945—the North Siders were bound to go on leaving their fans heartbroken.

Perhaps there was some truth in both. Or perhaps the real curse is believing in a curse at all. One thing we do know is this: The 2008 Cubs played some of the best baseball and provided some of the greatest thrills fans had

seen in a long time. Though they failed to reach their destination, the Cubs won more games than any other NL team and had a better home ledger (55–26) than any Cubs team since 1935 thanks to a stellar team effort and terrific chemistry amongst the players, including a record eight who were selected for the All-Star Game.

Chicago was the highest-scoring team in the National League with an order that produced from top to bottom. Eight Cubs who played 100 or more games hit .280 or better. Shortstop Ryan Theriot led the way at .307, with platoon players Mike Fontenot and Reed Johnson hitting .305 and .303, respectively. Six Cubs hit 20 or more home runs, led by Alfonso Soriano's 29.

On the mound, the Cubs had one of the best rotations in baseball and two reliable late relief men. Starters Ryan Dempster, Ted Lilly, and Carlos Zambrano won at least 14 games apiece, and midseason addition Rich Harden posted a 1.77 ERA. Set-up man Carlos Marmol was dependable at holding leads, and Kerry Wood (34 saves) made a successful transition to closer.

The Cubs won close games and blowouts. With their offense, no deficit ever seemed insurmountable. Their 184-run advantage over their opponents for the season was tops in the majors. By comparison, the Phillies were second in the NL with a 119-run differential.

But once again, it all unraveled in the playoffs as the Dodgers shut them down in three straight games, just as the Diamondbacks had done the year before. Fans were stunned as they watched their "Dream Team" self-destruct. **Mark DeRosa gave the Wrigley fans something to cheer about when he sent a two-run shot into the right-field bleachers**

in the second inning of Game 1. But then, Dempster, who'd won 17 games in the regular season, gave up seven walks and four runs in just 4⅔ innings. The Dodgers won 7–2.

Game 2 was no better as the Cubs went down 10–3. Zambrano, who'd pitched a no-hitter just a couple weeks before, gave up seven runs in 6⅓ innings. Four errors—one by each infielder—left the Cubbie faithful in stunned silence. Witnessing such incomprehensible doings, the fans were no doubt starting to wonder, "Maybe they are cursed."

In Los Angeles for Game 3, Harden gave up only three runs and the bullpen held the Dodgers close, but the Cubs' offense was able to muster just one run.

In the end, the 2008 season provided countless thrills for the Cubs and their fans, but destiny would have to wait.

BLEEDING CUBBIE BLUE

Ron Santo, a Seattle native and standout high school ballplayer, grew up watching the Cubs on TV and idolizing Ernie Banks. When each of the 16 major-league teams offered him a contract, he went with his heart and signed with the Cubs, even though their offer was lower than others. He simply felt that he was destined to play for the Chicago Cubs.

Santo debuted with the Cubs on June 26, 1960. At 6′0″ and 190 pounds, the 20-year-old rookie swung the bat for average and power, and he went on to anchor the hot corner for 14 years, becoming **one of the greatest offensive and defensive third basemen in the history of the game.**

As cleanup man in Chicago's lineup (between Hall of Famers Billy Williams and Banks), the nine-time All-Star could be counted on for 25 to 30 home runs and 90 to 100 RBI every season,

MAJOR LEAGUE TOTALS			
G	HR	RBI	BA
2,243	342	1,331	.277

in a period when few players reached either mark. His 1,290 RBI as a Cub rank fifth best on the team's all-time list, and his 337 homers rank fourth. A career .277 hitter, he batted or topped .300 four times.

Although Santo wasn't a natural third baseman, and he struggled to learn the position in the minors, he eventually became a standout defensively as well. He led all National League third basemen in assists for seven consecutive seasons and in putouts for six straight seasons (and seven overall), en route to five Gold Glove Awards.

What no one knew for years, however, was that, since age 18, Santo had been struggling with diabetes. In 1971, he finally went public with his struggle, and he immediately became a role model for children and adults with diabetes. That he was able to compete at such a high level and emerge as one of the very best while struggling with the disease on a daily basis is truly amazing.

Santo was such a true-blue Cub that when he was traded across town to the White Sox in 1974,

his heart wasn't in it, and he retired after his 15th major-league season. He just had too much Cubbie blue blood in his veins to adjust to the change.

Many fans, colleagues, and baseball historians believe that Santo should have been a shoo-in for the Hall of Fame—certainly his stats rank among the very best. In the meantime, **in 2003, the Cubs** bestowed on him their highest honor when they **retired his No. 10 jersey.**

Among the most popular players in franchise history, Santo has carved out a great second career in baseball, broadcasting for his beloved Cubs for almost 20 years, wearing his emotions on his sleeve, and unabashedly rooting for the Men in Blue. The diabetes he has battled most of his life has ravaged his health, but he is still loved by Chicago fans who will always consider him one of the best—even if the Hall of Fame never calls.

SEPTEMBER 28, 2003

Ron Santo

#10

"*I never did say you can't be a nice guy and win. I said that if I was playing third base and my mother rounded third with the winning run, I'd trip her.*"

—CUBS MANAGER LEO DUROCHER, EXPLAINING THE FAMOUS LINE ATTRIBUTED TO HIM: "NICE GUYS FINISH LAST."

DON'T MESS WITH "THE HAWK"

Andre Dawson crowded the plate. No debate there. He was hit by 111 pitches in his 21-year career, which ranks him among the top 50 in all-time totals. However, that does not exonerate Padres pitcher Eric Show for hitting "The Hawk" in the face with a fastball on July 7, 1987, causing a bloody gash that required 24 stitches to close.

Dawson had homered twice off the Padres the day before and went deep again in the first inning against Show. In "The Hawk's" next at-bat, Show **delivered a high heater that knocked him off his feet,** sent Cubs pitcher Rick Sutcliffe and others sprinting from the dugout, and ignited a brawl that emptied both benches.

After order was restored, Dawson got to his feet and went after Show, prompting a second scuffle in front of the Padres dugout. Both players were ejected, and the Cubs' Greg Maddux followed them out of the game after hitting Padres catcher Benito Santiago with a pitch in the fourth inning.

Show contended that the beaning was not intentional. Nevertheless, *Chicago Sun-Times* columnist Ron Rapoport called Show a "mediocre pitcher and a worse liar."

THE BARTMAN BALL

It could only have happened to the Cubs. The hand of fate was looking for some vessel to interfere with the Cubs' final push to the 2003 World Series. The Men in Blue led the best-of-seven National League Championship Series three games to two and seemed certain to win their first pennant in 58 years. Even after dropping Game 5 to the Marlins in Florida, it was assumed the Cubs would win one out of two games at Wrigley Field. This was the cruelest tease of all.

The lowlight of the collapse was the nearly incomprehensible doings in the eighth inning of Game 6 on October 14. The Cubs led 3–0. Starting pitcher Mark Prior seemed in complete command of the Florida batting order. Joy permeated the stands at Wrigley Field as he sent down Marlin after Marlin with little difficulty. The Cubs were five outs away from their first trip to the fall classic since 1945, and fans dared to ponder how they would obtain World Series tickets.

Trouble began when Marlin Luis Castillo sliced a pop fly down the third-base line to trigger **one of the most infamous moments in Cubs history.** Cubs left fielder Moises Alou ran for the stands, certain he could glove the ball in foul territory. Just as he reached up, so did a fan wearing a Cubs cap and headphones. The fan deflected the ball, which bounded away.

A livid Alou protested, shouted, and pleaded with the umpire to call fan interference, reasoning that he would have caught the ball if it weren't for the spectator. After that the Cubs self-destructed as Marlin after Marlin reached base and scored on their way to an 8–3 victory. That was merely a prelude to a Game 7 win and a trip to the World Series, which the Marlins eventually won.

Swiftly, the fan was hustled out of the park for his own safety. **Steve Bartman,** who was later identified as a committed Cubs supporter, **had only hoped for a souvenir,** but unwittingly became an instant villain. The 26-year-old fan became the object of intense scrutiny. His home and workplace were besieged by the media. Sarcastic trick-or-treaters actually dressed as him for Halloween just days after the playoffs ended.

Bartman kept a low profile. Undoubtedly shell-shocked by his leap into the limelight, he did not accept media invitations to talk about his fielding blunder, but he did issue a prepared statement, which, in part, read, "There are few words to describe how awful I feel.... I've been a Cub fan all my life and fully understand the relationship between my actions and the outcome of the game." Bartman said he never thought the ball would be in play and didn't see Alou coming because he was watching the sky for the ball.

Bartman did not even get to keep the most infamous foul ball in Cubs history. A Chicago attorney scooped it up and auctioned it off. Harry Caray's Restaurant bought the ball for more than $100,000, displayed it, then held a highly publicized event to blow it up.

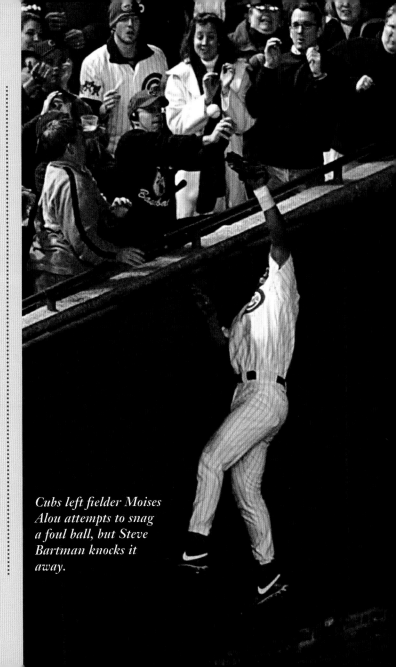

Cubs left fielder Moises Alou attempts to snag a foul ball, but Steve Bartman knocks it away.

EAMUS CATULI!

Outside the right-field wall of Wrigley Field, mounted on a brick building across Sheffield Avenue, is a sign posted by the Lakeview Baseball Club reading "Eamus Catuli!" Loosely translated from Latin, the phrase means, "Let's Go Cubs!"

A second sign, using a mix of letters and numbers, tells a sad story. The two letters at the front end are AC. They stand for "Anno Catuli" or "In the year of the Cub." The following six digits represent how many years it has been since the Cubs won a division title, a pennant, and a World Series championship.

"The last time the Cubs won a World Series was in 1908. The last time they were in one was 1945. Hey, any team can have a bad century."

—FORMER CUBS MANAGER TOM TREBELHORN

MORDECAI "THREE-FINGER" BROWN

Mordecai Peter Centennial "Three-Finger" Brown earned his nickname rather painfully. He lost two fingers on his right (pitching) hand in a childhood farm accident.

No one used the word *disability* when Brown reached the major leagues in 1903 with the St. Louis Cardinals, who were not wise enough to hang on to the hurler after one mediocre season and allowed him to slip away to the Cubs. Throwing **a virtually unhittable curveball,** Brown won 15 or more games for the Cubs eight times, including a franchise-record 29 in 1908. During the 1906 season he also recorded a miniscule earned run average of 1.04, breathtaking in its stinginess.

When Brown retired after 14 years in the big leagues, including a stay from 1904 to 1912 with the Cubs (plus a career wrap-up cameo in 1916), he had a record of 239–130 (a .648 winning percentage) and an earned run average of 2.06.

His statistical magnificence, which led to his induction in the Hall of Fame in 1949, gave Brown more than ample ammunition when facing even the best of sluggers.

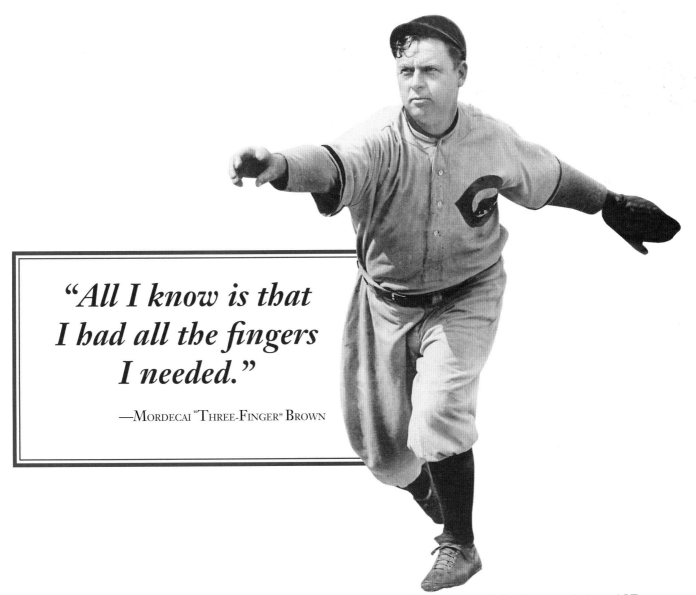

> *"All I know is that I had all the fingers I needed."*

—MORDECAI "THREE-FINGER" BROWN

PHIL CAVARRETTA

Phil Cavarretta was the local boy who made good for the Cubs. Within a few months, the young infielder went from Lane Tech High School on Chicago's north side to the Cubs roster with only a very brief stop in Class A in between.

Cavarretta, a first baseman who began his 22-year major-league career in 1934, got the call from the Cubs at the tail end of the season and, **in his first plate appearance, smacked a home run.** He was still only 18 years old. During a career in which he played 20 straight seasons with the Cubs (his last two seasons were with the White Sox), Cavarretta appeared in 2,030 games.

As a four-time All-Star, Cavarretta led the National League in batting in 1945 with a .355 average and was the team's chief offensive weapon in the run for the pennant that year. Never a huge home run threat, Cavarretta stroked just 95 in his career but drove in 820 runs and had a lifetime batting average of .293.

Cavarretta said **the only thing he wanted to do in life was grow up to play for the Cubs.** At age 77, he indicated that his allegiance hadn't wavered. "I'm still a Cub. Always was, always will be."

> *"I played with the Cubs for 20 years.*
> *But our 1935 club was the best ballclub*
> *I played on with the Cubs."*

—Phil Cavarretta

The 1935 Chicago Cubs. (Left to right): *Augie Galan, Billy Herman, Fred Lindstrom, Gabby Hartnett, Frank Demaree, Phil Cavarretta, Stan Hack, Billy Jurges, Lon Warneke, and Charlie Grimm*

D-LEE

Acquiring first baseman Derrek Lee in 2004 was one of the great Cubs coups of recent years. The nephew of former major-leaguer Leron Lee, Derrek was so good around the first sack that he reminded fans of Mark Grace.

Lee also emerged as a huge offensive asset. In 2005, he led the National League with a .335 batting average while stroking 50 doubles and 46 home runs en route to 107 RBI. Besides winning the batting title, Lee also won the Silver Slugger Award as the best-hitting first baseman in the league that year. And his candor and pleasant personality made him an instant hit with teammates and Cubs fans alike.

How important D-Lee became to the Cubs was evident when a 2006 injury limited him to just 50 games. The team was unable to adjust to his absence from the lineup. A wrist injury in 2007 held down his home run production, but D-Lee was back at full strength for the 2008 season, and his 20 home runs and 90 RBI helped the Cubs return to the playoffs for a second straight year.

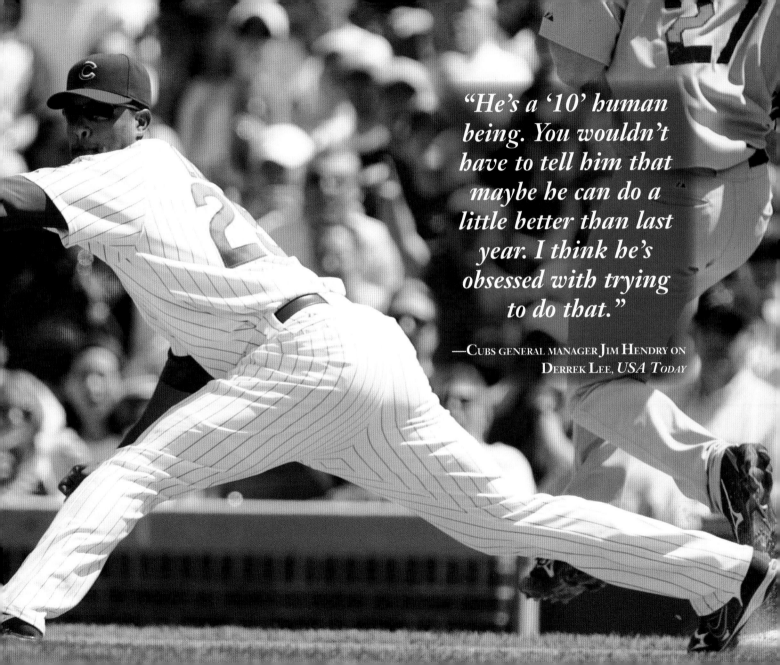

"He's a '10' human being. You wouldn't have to tell him that maybe he can do a little better than last year. I think he's obsessed with trying to do that."

—CUBS GENERAL MANAGER JIM HENDRY ON DERREK LEE, *USA TODAY*

JUST CALL HIM "SARGE"

Although he returned to the Cubs as a coach under the Dusty Baker regime, Gary Matthews is most closely identified with the 1984 team that earned the Cubs a spot in the postseason for the first time in 39 years. Matthews spent three-plus years of his 16-season major-league career with the Cubs, but '84 was the special one.

While playing in Philadelphia, Pete Rose, the all-time hits leader, christened Matthews "Sarge" for his take-charge demeanor in the clubhouse. When Dallas Green, who managed the Phillies to a World Series title in 1980, went to the Cubs as general manager after the 1981 season, he stocked up on ex-Phillies and acquired Matthews before the '84 season.

In 1984, Matthews batted .291 with 14 homers and 82 RBI, walked 103 times, and led the league in on-base percentage (.410). The Cubs felt they had beaten the curse when they led the San Diego Padres two games to none in the National League Championship Series, but then they lost three straight.

BOYS WILL BE BOYS

When Mother Nature turned the first scheduled night game at Wrigley Field into an outdoor shower after 3½ innings on August 8, 1988, a few of the Cubs players turned the rainout into a scene from the movie *Bull Durham*.

Reenacting the scene where Kevin Costner leads his Durham Bulls teammates in headfirst slides across the drenched tarp covering the infield, **catcher Jody Davis and pitchers Greg Maddux, Al Nipper, and Les Lancaster were among the Cubs who went slip-sliding away.**

Cubs general manager Jim Frey was not amused by the stunt. He fined the players a modest $500 apiece. Davis said the outrage from Cubs management centered mostly on the team's young ace.

"They said, 'You could have caused a riot, and Maddux could have gotten hurt,'" Davis recalled 20 years later.

Greg Maddux slides across the rain-soaked tarp as Les Lancaster looks on.

Chip, Harry, and Skip Caray

A TRIO OF CARAYS

The descendants of Harry Caray followed his vocal chords into the broadcast booth, defying the adage that he would be an impossible act to follow. Son Skip Caray became the radio broadcaster for the Atlanta Braves in 1976. Skip's son Chip followed his dad and grandfather into the booth, working as an announcer for FOX Sports before spending 1998–2004 with the Cubs and then joining the Braves' broadcast team.

On May 13, 1991, all three Carays worked the broadcast booth for a game between the Braves and Cubs, with the two younger Carays on the Braves' side of the wall.

> ## *"It might be...*
> ## *it could be...*
> ## *it is...*
> ## *a home run!"*

> —Harry Caray's famous
> HOME RUN CALL

Memorable Home Runs in Cubs History

- Gabby Hartnett's legendary "Homer in the Gloamin'" came on September 28, 1938, during the ninth inning in a darkening Wrigley Field, giving the Cubs a 6–5 win over the Pirates and boosting them into first place by half a game.

- Ernie Banks smacked his 500th major-league home run on May 12, 1970, against the Braves at Wrigley Field.

- On September 27, 1930, Hack Wilson hit his 56th home run of the season, setting a National League single-season record that stood until 1998.

- On September 25, 1998, Sammy Sosa's 66th home run established a new single-season record for the Cubs but came in a loss to the Astros in Houston.

- On May 11, 2000, Glenallen Hill crushed a ball an estimated 550 feet. It landed on the roof of a five-story apartment building on Waveland and Kenmore across the street from the ballpark in what may have been the longest home run ever hit at Wrigley Field.

- Joe Tinker's eighth-inning home run on October 11, 1908, was a key blow in the Cubs' win over the Detroit Tigers in the second game of the World Series. Because this was the dead-ball era, Tinker's shot was also the first home run hit in the World Series in five years.

- During a May 5, 1996, victory over the New York Mets, Sammy Sosa hit a blast over Wrigley's left-field wall that broke a second-floor window in an apartment building on Waveland Avenue. Imagine the surprise when the homeowner returned from work.... "Those darn kids!"

- Suffering from blurred vision while in the throws of a diabetic episode, Ron Santo smashed a game-winning grand slam into Wrigley's left-field bleachers to beat the Dodgers 4–1 on September 25, 1968.

- On October 5, 2003, Alex Gonzalez and Aramis Ramirez each cracked a home run to beat Atlanta 5–1 as the Cubs won their first postseason series since the 1908 World Series.

- Aramis Ramirez cranked a first-inning grand slam on October 11, 2003, as the Cubs defeated the Florida Marlins 8–3 to take a three-games-to-one lead in the National League Championship Series.

- On October 2, 1984, Cubs pitcher Rick Sutcliffe hit a surprise home run in the first game of the National League Championship Series. The Cubs beat the San Diego Padres that day 13–0.

- Augie Galan's grand slam to spark an 8–2 win over the Phillies on September 4, 1935, provided the first victory in the Cubs' 21-game winning streak. The Cubs clinched the pennant during that illustrious stretch.

- On September 28, 1998, Gary Gaetti hit a two-run homer to lead the Cubs to a 5–3 victory over the Giants in a one-game playoff to determine the Wild Card winner, thus allowing the North Siders to advance to the Division Series.

- On October 2, 2001, Sammy Sosa hit his 60th dinger of the season, making him the first player in major-league history to hit 60 or more home runs per season three times during his career.

GROVER CLEVELAND ALEXANDER

Grover Cleveland "Old Pete" Alexander had difficulties with alcohol, but that didn't stop him from becoming **one of the greatest pitchers in baseball history.** Alexander, who three times won 30 or more games with the Philadelphia Phillies, served the Cubs nobly from 1918 to 1926.

Alexander's best year for Chicago was 1920, when he went 27–14 with a 1.91 ERA. He led the National League in wins that year, as well as starts, with 40 (he also pitched some in relief), and complete games with 33. And although his numbers were not as glittery as they had been with the Phils, Alexander also won 22 games for the Cubs in 1923 and 15 or more games four other times. Alexander's career total of 373 victories is tied for third on the all-time major-league list.

Long after he retired, an actor by the name of Ronald Reagan—on his way to greater fame in another, more high-profile job—portrayed Alexander in a 1952 movie about his life called *The Winning Team.*

SPRING TRAINING ON CUBBIE ISLAND

Spring training—a time for players to limber up their legs under the warm sun and for fans to enjoy the sights, sounds, and smells of baseball's return. Rarely has the paradise of spring training been so tangible as when the **Cubs called Catalina Island their February and March home** from 1921 to '51, except for a few years during World War II when they trained in French Lick, Indiana.

Team owner William Wrigley, Jr., purchased the largely undeveloped island 25 miles off the Los Angeles coast in 1919 for $3 million. Amid its eucalyptus trees and mountains, he built a ballpark to the dimensions of Chicago's Wrigley Field and made it the gorgeous spring training home of the North Siders.

If the scenery and luxurious accommodations at the Catalina Country Club did not inspire hard work, the morning runs through the rugged mountain terrain made up for it. And while the players toiled under the sun, Catalina Island became a popular vacation destination for Chicagoans, even after the Cubs moved their spring training home to Mesa, Arizona, in 1952, when the need to find more exhibition opponents outweighed the allure of an island paradise for baseball.

Like soldiers going off to battle, the Cubs march into spring training escorted by drummers from the Catalina Post of the American Legion.

1998: CHASING THE DREAM

For Cubs fans, the 1997 season was depressing from start to finish. The team went 0–14 to start the year, finished 68–94 overall, and was mired in the cellar of the National League Central Division. Then, during the off-season, beloved broadcaster Harry Caray passed away. How much worse could things get? There weren't many predictions going into the 1998 season, even from true believers, who always feel the Cubs are going to erupt with a rash of victories. Baseball itself was still suffering from lingering fan anger because of the 1994 labor strike that resulted in the cancellation of the World Series.

Few expected the Cubs to play a significant role in the resurrection of the sport, but they did just that. Wildly popular right fielder Sammy Sosa and St. Louis Cardinals first baseman Mark McGwire engaged in a two-man chase of Roger Maris's 37-year-old, single-season home-run record of 61. They generated so much excitement in their quest, with the more gregarious Sosa bringing McGwire out of his shell in a feel-good story, that the pennant races were overshadowed.

The home run race was perhaps a useful diversion, taking pressure off the team. But for the 1998 Chicago Cubs, the pennant chase was a team effort. Right-handed pitcher **Kevin Tapani rose to the occasion,** winning 19 games and slugging a grand slam in one of

them. Reliever Rod Beck saved 51 games in 81 appearances. And a young Kerry Wood startled fans with a 20-strikeout game in May and won Rookie of the Year honors, too.

But after 162 games, the Cubs and the Giants were essentially in the same spot as they were on Opening Day. Cubs fans crossed their fingers. This was typical of the team. Bring fans to the brink and then break their hearts. Not this time. The Cubs advanced to the postseason as they bested the Giants 5–3 in a one-game playoff for the Wild Card spot, boosted by **Gary Gaetti's pivotal two-run homer** and stellar pitching by Steve Trachsel, who allowed just one hit in 6⅓ innings.

Although a superior Atlanta Braves team, featuring, of course, former Cub Greg Maddux, swept the Men in Blue in the Division Series, fans were glowing over the unexpected gift of a season. The team had jumped from 68 wins in 1997 to 90 a year later and possessed just about the most exciting player in the game on its roster.

RICK SUTCLIFFE
THE RED BARON

In the middle of the 1984 season, Rick Sutcliffe was minding his own business with the Cleveland Indians (though not as well as he would have liked with a 4–5 record), when his career was forever transformed.

On June 13, the Cubs and Indians completed a seven-player deal that sent Sutcliffe to the Windy City. The tall redhead had **a delivery that was far from picturesque,** sometimes throwing like a windup toy running out of steam, but his pitches never did. Sutcliffe embarked on a stunning run, going 16–1 for the Cubs over the rest of the regular season, with a 2.69 ERA. Despite spending the first two and half months of the season in the American League, Sutcliffe was so good that he won the National League Cy Young Award.

Sutcliffe, who later became a nationally respected broadcaster with ESPN, had other excellent years for the Cubs, winning 18 games in 1987 and 16 in 1989 before being shipped off to the Baltimore Orioles and then the St. Louis Cardinals, where he culminated his 18-year major-league career in 1994.

CUBS QUIZ

1. What was manager **Leo Durocher's** most famous nickname?

. . . .

2. What pitcher led the Cubs in victories the first three years of the 1950s?

. . . .

3. What pitcher led the Cubs in victories the last three years of the 1970s?

. . . .

4. **Rogers Hornsby** was perhaps the greatest right-handed hitter of all-time. What was his nickname?

. . . .

5. Who hit the most grand slams, and how many, in a Cubs uniform?

. . . .

6. After the 2003 season, he was traded from the Marlins to the Cubs for Hee Seop Choi. Incidently, his father is the scout who originally signed Choi to the Cubs. Who is he?

. . . .

1. "Leo the Lip"; 2. Bob Rush; 3. Rick Reuschel—20, 14, 18; 4. The Rajah; 5. Ernie Banks—12; 6. Derrek Lee

Alfonso Soriano

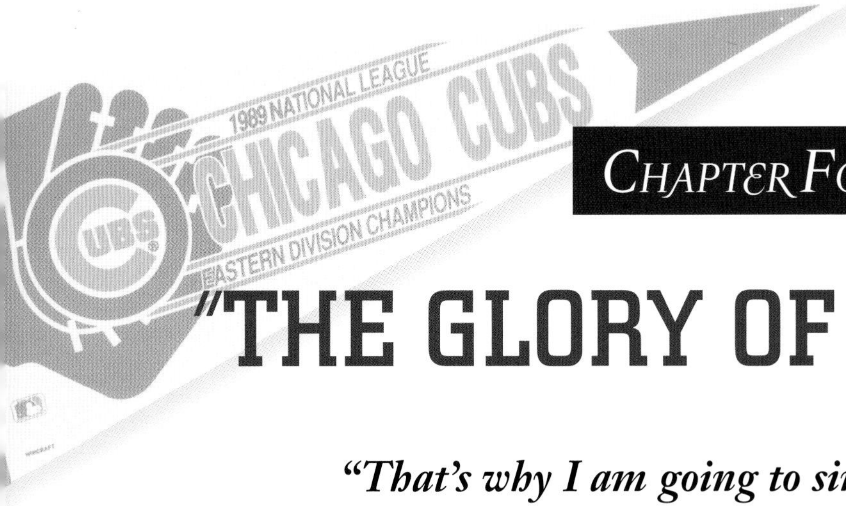

CHAPTER FOUR

"THE GLORY OF THE CUBS"

"That's why I am going to sing this song to you,

For I know it is true,

The Cubs have won the champion game,

Won it fair, I declare, no one is to blame.

The crowds are cheering them with joy and glee,

Each heart as happy as can be.

But now the season's over, they have laid down their clubs.

It's the glory of the Cubs."

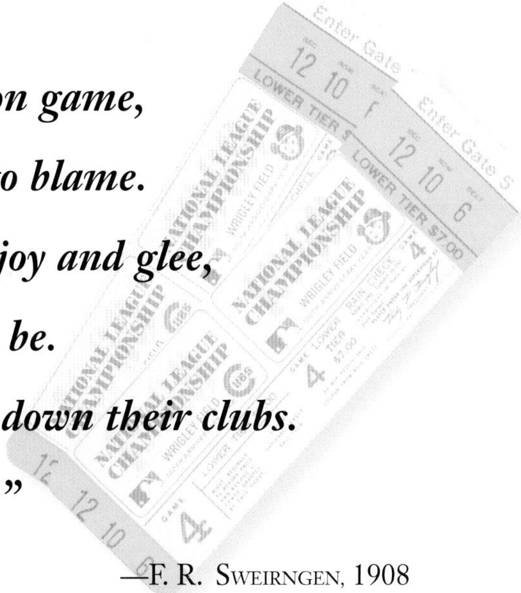

—F. R. SWEIRNGEN, 1908

*"There is so much hunger in those fans to win a World Series
and each time you make it to the playoffs, they think
you're going to do it and end the wait."*

—MARK GRACE, 1998

CAJUN CONNECTION CLICKS
"THE RIOT" AND "LITTLE BABE RUTH"

If Ryan Theriot and Mike Fontenot seem to have a special chemistry as a double-play combination, there's a good reason for it. Call it Louisiana luck.

Theriot and Fontenot were the starting shortstop and second baseman, respectively, on the LSU team that won the 2000 College World Series. The Louisiana natives had not played together since then until Fontenot was called up from the minors in June 2007. Both were 2001 draftees—Fontenot by the Orioles and Theriot by the Cubs. Fontenot came to the Cubs in the Sammy Sosa trade before the 2005 season and played 86 games in the majors after his '07 call-up.

The Bayou Boys' reunion helped the Cubs to a spicy 2008. With Fontenot sharing time with Mark DeRosa, the second base position produced clutch hitting and solid defense. Fontenot's timely hits and .305 season average even prompted Ron Santo to nickname him "Little Babe Ruth."

Ryan Theriot and Mike Fontenot

Meanwhile, Theriot enjoyed a career season at shortstop with 178 hits, a .307 batting average, and a .975 fielding percentage.

Down on the Delta, surely they were celebrating cajun-style.

LIFE IN THE BLEACHERS

If Wrigley Field represents the soul of the Chicago Cubs, then **the bleachers represent the soul of Wrigley Field.**

There was a time when the bleachers were the cheap seats—not the best seats in the house but a place that captured the essence of baseball at its purest. It only cost a buck to enter and experience the thrill of a major-league baseball game and the magic of Wrigley Field.

In the modern era of baseball, where the price of everything rises parallel to the price of hiring ballplayers, bleacher seats are no longer the best deal in the house—far from it. Yet they retain their well-earned reputation for fun in the sun and a pretty good chance to snag a long ball, especially when the wind obliges by blowing out. This is where fans are most likely to strip off T-shirts to work on their tans; where the most brazen might have the letters C-U-B-S painted on their chests. **It's where signs declaring Cubs love are held the highest.**

While the bleachers are certainly viewed as a place to party, they are also home to some of the most knowledgeable and most ardent fans—"Bleacher Bums" with memories and statistics embedded in their minds. They do not quite have squatters' rights to their seats—nearly all the seats are first come, first serve—but it seems they do. You'll find many of them in the same place throughout the season (throughout the years, in many cases), watching the action unfold from their constant perch.

And yes, the bleachers are still a place where opinions—and beer—flow freely and where Cubs fans young and old enjoy the thrill of the game in their very own little neighborhood of the Friendly Confines—and they continue to sell out at every home game.

"I'd always thought of Wrigley Field's bleachers as the place where real baseball fans go when they close their eyes and click their heels three times."

—AUTHOR LONNIE WHEELER, BLEACHERS: A SUMMER IN WRIGLEY FIELD

RYAN DEMPSTER
COMIC RELIEF

Right-handed pitcher Ryan Dempster dabbles in **stand-up comedy** in nightclubs during his free time, but during spring training in 2008, he wasn't joking when he predicted the Cubs' first World Series title in 100 years. The Cubs moved Dempster from the bullpen to the starting rotation in 2008, and his first-half numbers got him elected to the All-Star team. He went 10–4 in the first half of the season, winning all ten of those games at Wrigley Field while suffering only one loss at the Friendly Confines. He finished the season 17–6 with 14 wins and only three losses at home and led the starting five in innings pitched (206.2) and strikeouts (187).

"We rag on each other, have fun, and it keeps us loose. The more relaxed you are, the better you're going to perform."

—CUBS PITCHER RYAN DEMPSTER ON THE INTERACTION BETWEEN RELIEF PITCHERS, FROM *ENTANGLED IN IVY* BY GEORGE CASTLE

"Even though you know you are an All-Star and you have done some good things, just to see your name on that locker alongside some of the others is just something you will never forget."

—Pitcher Rick Sutcliffe on the honor of being elected to the All-Star team, from *Cubs: Where Have You Gone?* by Fred Mitchell

Stand-ins for Harry Caray While He Recuperated from a Stroke in 1987

- Sportscaster Brent Musburger

- Actor Bill Murray

  - Actor George Wendt

  - Actor Jim Belushi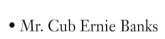

  - Actor Dan Aykroyd

  - Sportscaster Bob Costas

  - Longtime Detroit Tigers broadcaster Ernie Harwell

- Sportscaster Dick Enberg

- TV personality Bryant Gumbel

- Sportscaster Gary Bender

- Longtime St. Louis Cardinals broadcaster Jack Buck

- Mr. Cub Ernie Banks

- Newspaper columnist Mike Royko

- Newspaper columnist George Will

  - Legendary Cardinals slugger Stan Musial

  - Sportscaster Pat Summerall

KESSINGER AND BECKERT
THE DYNAMIC DUO

For most of a decade, the names Kessinger and Beckert were always uttered in the same sentence, as if they were partners at the same law firm. In their case, they would have specialized as defense attorneys.

From 1964 to 1975, **Don Kessinger took the field at shortstop** 1,618 times for the Cubs (more than any shortstop in team history), pairing with scrappy **SECOND BASEMAN GLENN BECKERT** (1,206 games) from 1965 to 1973. After nine years of working in tandem, the pair was as synchronized as Fred Astaire and Ginger Rogers, if not quite as rhythmic, as they defended the middle infield for the Cubs.

Together, six-time All-Star Kessinger and four-time All-Star Beckert were greater than their individual parts. They knew each other's strengths and limitations and parlayed that knowledge into hundreds of double plays. Of course, no matter their chemistry together, it certainly didn't hurt that the Cubs fielded the same infield for five straight years, increasing the camaraderie and surrounding the double-play duo with superstars Ernie Banks at first and Ron Santo at the hot corner.

Don Kessinger finishes off a double-play as Glenn Beckert looks on.

RYNE SANDBERG
KID NATURAL

MAJOR LEAGUE TOTALS			
G	HR	RBI	BA
2,164	282	1,061	.285

Deemed a "throw-in" in the 1982 Ivan DeJesus–Larry Bowa swap with the Phillies, Ryne Sandberg yielded a pretty good return for the Cubs.

A strong all-around athlete from Spokane, Washington, Sandberg was drafted by Philly in 1978, but he saw little action in the majors before Cubs GM (and former Phillies manager) Dallas Green stole him away, insisting that the little-known infielder be included in the '82 deal.

Originally installed at third, Ryno was moved to second base the following year, and he immediately won the first of his nine consecutive Gold Gloves. As a second baseman, Sandberg possessed the rare combination of fielding prowess (his career .989 fielding percentage is a major-league record at second base), surprising power (he slugged as many as 40 home runs in a season), and the ability to hit for average (he batted over .300 on five occasions).

Ryno came to be regarded as the supreme professional—a man of character who came to work every day and did his job with excellence more than flair. Sandberg took the game seriously, and fans embraced him on his terms. It was the quality of his work and his demeanor on and off the field that made him one of the most beloved Cubs of all time. And his breakout season in 1984 didn't hurt. As the team won its first-ever NL East title, the league MVP notched 200 hits, 36 doubles, 19 triples, 19 homers, and 84 RBI, combined with 32 steals, a .314 average, and stellar defense.

The defining game of that MVP season, and of Sandberg's career, was his five-hit, two-home run, seven-RBI monster performance on June 23, 1984, in which he led the Cubs to a nationally televised extra-inning win over the St. Louis Cardinals. All told, he emerged from "The Sandberg Game" an MLB superstar.

For most of the next 13 years, the future Hall of Famer was a picture of excellence and consistency on the field. After leading the Cubs back to the playoffs in '89, the ten-time All-Star retired (in 1994—and again in '97) with 2,386 hits, 403 doubles, 344 steals, and 1,318 runs scored—including a then-record 282 homers as a second baseman.

In 2005, Sandberg was elected to the Hall of Fame and the Cubs retired his No. 23 jersey. In his acceptance speech, in typical Ryno fashion, he spoke out for the integrity of the game. It was a speech emblematic of the man. No frivolity, all seriousness—spoken from the heart, it got the job done. And that is how Cubs fans will always remember Ryne Sandberg.

> Ryno's last game at Wrigley Field came on September 21, 1997, which, coincidentally, was also the last game in which Sandberg supporter and friend Harry Caray would sing "Take Me Out to the Ball Game" during the seventh-inning stretch. (Caray died the following off-season.)

ANTONIO ALFONSECA
PITCHER WITH A DOZEN DIGITS

When Antonio Alfonseca bumped umpire Justin Klemm during an argument in 2003, Cubs manager Dusty Baker called it "assault with a deadly belly."

Relief pitcher Antonio Alfonseca hails from the Dominican Republic. He is 6'5", and when he came to the Cubs from the Florida Marlins in 2002, his weight was listed at 250 pounds. He also has **six fingers on each hand and six toes on each foot,** a condition known as polydactylism. But like Mordecai Brown, whose pitching was not *adversely* affected because he had only three fingers on his pitching hand, there is no evidence to suggest that Alfonseca's pitching was *enhanced* by having an extra finger. Cubs fans would probably agree with that sentiment.

PHILLIES 23, CUBS 22

Major League Baseball can look a lot like slow-pitch softball when the wind blows out at Wrigley Field. Such was the case on May 17, 1979, when the Phillies outlasted the Cubs by a 23–22 score on Mike Schmidt's home run in the tenth inning.

When **each starting pitcher recorded just one out,** the 14,952 fans in attendance knew this would be no quick game. Chicago's Dennis Lamp surrendered six runs on six hits in his ⅓ inning, and Philadelphia's Randy Lerch yielded five runs on five hits in the same duration.

The teams combined for 50 hits, including 11 home runs—six for the Cubs and five for the Phillies. Dave Kingman went deep three times for Chicago. Schmidt's long ball in the tenth was his second of the game.

It took 4 hours, 3 minutes to complete and was the highest-scoring game in the majors since 1922, when the Cubs won a 26–23 slugfest also against the Phillies.

HOLY COW!
THE LEGENDARY HARRY CARAY

Harry Caray swashbuckled through life. It just so happened that much of that time was spent on the air, where he broadcasted baseball games and sprinkled the time between pitches and at-bats with tidbits of philosophy about life and baseball.

"Holy Cow!" was what Caray shouted in the press box each time he saw something that impressed him on the baseball field. And that occurred just often enough to keep his audience laughing and coming back for more.

Actually, Caray's bigger-than-life persona was fed by **a general view that life was too short, so you'd better have a good time.** "Booze, broads, and BS," he said. "If you got that, what else do you need?"

Apparently, a broadcasting forum. Caray winged his way through baseball broadcasts for the St. Louis Cardinals, Chicago White Sox, and Oakland A's before he settled into Wrigley Field decades into his career. It just took that long to find the perfect match.

In 1976, when White Sox owner Bill Veeck overheard Caray singing "Take Me Out to the Ball Game" during the seventh-inning stretch of a game, he cajoled his broadcaster into leading the fans in a rendition of the song. By the time he arrived at Wrigley Field in 1982, he had the routine perfected. He was a bandleader with a microphone, a gravelly voiced singer with the world's largest backup choir.

On the air, Harry told it like it was, sometimes to the point of angering Cubs players. He wore glasses the size of windowpanes, allowing for easy parody. He hugged every woman who walked by. He mangled names on the air—even pronouncing them backward just for the fun of it. He delivered messages from fans while broadcasting partners scrambled to keep listeners informed of the action. And yet, he was more beloved than most of the players he covered.

Caray entertained on the air, and then after hours, too, touring the clubs of Rush Street (and anywhere else that was open late), where he embraced the people who embraced him. He was always on, always having a blast, a pied piper who could create a crowd merely with his presence and get it to follow him anywhere.

Harry Caray was a broad-brush sportscaster who painted in vivid colors, while allowing others to fill in the numbers. He was a magic man with a microphone who held onto an audience even when the Cubs failed to hold onto the lead. He was the king of showmanship for a team that often lacked a quality showman on the field. In his own way, Caray was as optimistic about baseball and the Cubs as the ever-sunny Ernie Banks.

Harry Caray died in 1998, but his spirit lives on with Cubs fans, who can now admire a statue of him outside Wrigley Field and a caricature of him above the broadcast booth that he called home for so many years.

"Hello again, everybody," Harry would say at the onset of a broadcast. "It's a bee-yooo-tiful day for baseball."

And whether it was cloudy, windy, or cold, Harry was always right.

BILL VEECK, SR.

As a caustic sportswriter for the *Chicago American*, Bill Veeck, Sr., regularly criticized Cubs operations—until team owner William Wrigley, Jr., challenged him to prove he could do a better job running the team. Veeck took him up on the offer and became team president in July 1919. Steady and smart, calm and uncontroversial—and utterly committed to the success of the franchise—Veeck overhauled the team's roster and led the Cubs to three pennants during his term. He remained in the position until his death in 1933, and, along the way, he tutored his son Bill Veeck, Jr., in the art of fan friendliness—a move that paid off later when the junior Veeck became a team owner.

HATS OFF TO BIITTNER

If you were keeping score at home, you might have jotted down "Cap–9–5."

On September 26, 1979, Larry Biittner was playing right field for the Cubs. During the top of the fourth, his cap flew off his head while chasing a fly ball hit by the Mets' Bruce Boisclair. Unfortunately for Biittner, the loose lid fell right on top of the ball, concealing it from his view as the fans in the bleachers bellowed, "Hat! Hat! Hat!"

The vocal assist from the fans gave the story a happy ending for the Cubs. Biittner located the ball and threw out Boisclair at third base.

It might have been the most embarrassing play of Biittner's 14-year major-league career, but it was not his only legacy. He batted .290 during that '79 campaign, and two years prior, he hit .298 with 12 homers for the Cubs.

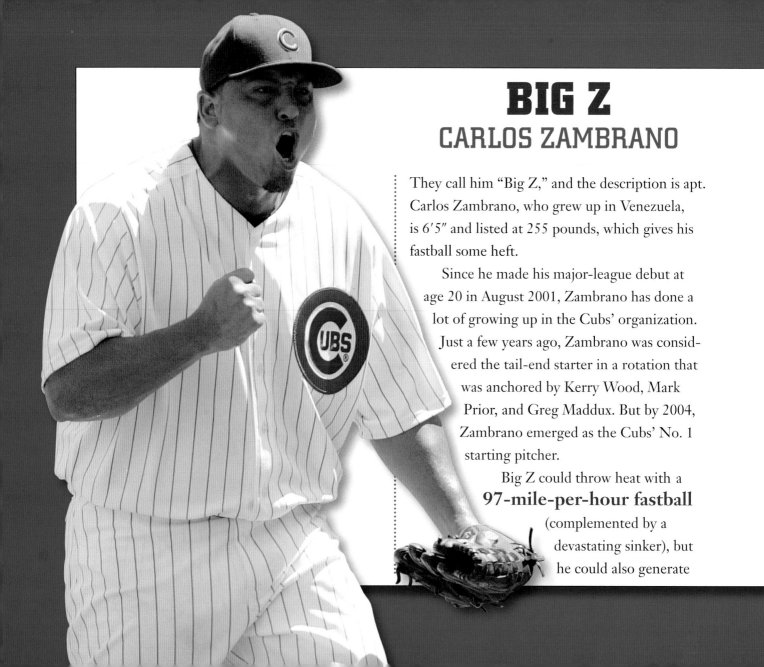

BIG Z
CARLOS ZAMBRANO

They call him "Big Z," and the description is apt. Carlos Zambrano, who grew up in Venezuela, is 6'5" and listed at 255 pounds, which gives his fastball some heft.

Since he made his major-league debut at age 20 in August 2001, Zambrano has done a lot of growing up in the Cubs' organization. Just a few years ago, Zambrano was considered the tail-end starter in a rotation that was anchored by Kerry Wood, Mark Prior, and Greg Maddux. But by 2004, Zambrano emerged as the Cubs' No. 1 starting pitcher.

Big Z could throw heat with a **97-mile-per-hour fastball** (complemented by a devastating sinker), but he could also generate heat on the field and in the clubhouse. Opponents didn't like it when a strikeout sent Carlos into a fist-pumping celebration. They thought he was showing them up. Zambrano said it was just his natural enthusiasm.

Whether it is a smile when the side goes down 1–2–3 or a frown when a ball is struck fair, **it doesn't take a detective to read Zambrano's emotions.** He would make a better living as a mime than a poker player.

In 2007, when Zambrano and catcher Michael Barrett had a disagreement that led to punches being thrown, it was Barrett who not only went home with the bruises but also went bye-bye from the organization.

Zambrano also ran into games where he suffered cramps from dehydration and had to leave the mound, scaring fans who worried that he was injured. He admitted to drinking too much coffee, so his coaches advised him to cut down on his caffeine intake and urged him to drink more water or an energy drink. If Gatorade made coffee-flavored sports drinks, Big Z would be set.

Among the minority of pitchers who consider the use of a bat to be of more help than a toothpick, Zambrano takes pride in his hitting. **Playing in the National League with no designated hitter, he has won a Silver Slugger Award for his position.** In 2006, Zambrano hit six home runs (more than some middle infielders) to equal the single-season team record for pitchers set by Ferguson Jenkins in 1971. With four homers in 2008, he surpassed Jenkins as the pitcher with the most home runs as a Cub.

During the 2007 season, Zambrano's contract situation became a soap opera until he signed a $91.5-million deal that carries him through 2012. Now with seasons of 13, 16, 14, 16, 18, and 14 wins on his résumé, including a no-hitter in 2008 (not to mention a .337 batting average), no one doubts that **Big Z is the ace of the Cubs' rotation.**

JIM EDMONDS
NO LONGER A CUB KILLER

May 15, 2008, was a strange afternoon for Jim Edmonds. For the first time in his career, he was cheered when he raced to his center-field position at Wrigley Field.

Edmonds, an eight-time Gold Glove winner whose spectacular defense and productive bat helped the St. Louis Cardinals to six playoff appearances, two NL pennants, and a 2006 World Series title, was always the enemy in the "Friendly Confines." He was routinely subjected to boos, jeers, and R-rated language from the Bleacher Bums.

But here was Edmonds, getting a hit in his Cubs debut to kickstart a season in which he helped the Cubs outdistance his former team in the standings while platooning in center field with Reed Johnson. And actually hearing cheers!

"It was a little different," admitted Edmonds, who broke in with the Angels in 1993, spent eight years in St. Louis, and opened '08 with the Padres before he was released and picked up by the Cubs.

"I've always admired this ballpark, and this team, and wanted to see what it was like on this side one time."

During 2008, Edmonds solidified the Cubs' center-field defense, brought pennant-race experience to the clubhouse, and put himself within striking range of 400 career home runs. He hit .319 in June, with a .667 slugging percentage, while sparking the Cubs to one of the best seasons in their history.

> Edmonds, a four-time All-Star, won a Silver Slugger Award in 2004, when he hit .301 with 111 RBI and tied his career high with 42 home runs.

KING KONG

Nicknamed "King Kong," Dave Kingman was a poor fielder and generally wasn't considered a nice person. But boy, could he slug the ball. When he stepped into the batter's box with the Cubs from 1978 to 1980, fans held their breath. And when the hard-hitting slugger hit 48 long balls to lead the league in 1979 (twice hitting three home runs in a game), Cubs fans cheered him on. But with an unpleasant attitude and a league-leading 131 strikeouts (also in '79), the slugger was surly and unpredictable, and he never kept friends for long.

Home run or strikeout, that was Kingman, on and off the field.

> In 1976, Kingman blasted one out of Wrigley, over Waveland Avenue, and off a house on Kenmore Avenue. Unfortunately for the Cubs, he was playing for the Mets at the time.

MAJOR LEAGUE TOTALS			
BA	**HR**	**RBI**	**SO**
.236	442	1,210	1,816

SUPERSTITIOUS CUBS

Cubs Hall of Fame infielder and manager Frank Chance wrote in a 1913 *New York Times* article, **"Possibly no other ball club in the country ever boasted as many superstitious fellows as the Chicago Cubs."**

Chance himself was among those fellows, and the parade of North Side quirkiness has not stopped in the decades since. Here are some Cubs rituals over the years.

Frank Chance—On trains, "The Peerless Leader" always occupied berth No. 13, saying "a number so frequently dodged by the average traveler has been a lucky charm to me."

Harry Steinfeldt—Refused to have his soiled undershirt washed if the Cubs were in the midst of a winning streak.

Billy Williams—Would spit when coming up to the plate, then hit the gob of spit with his bat.

Leo Durocher—Is said to have once worn the same jacket, slacks, and tie for three and a half weeks out of fear that changing clothes would trigger bad luck.

Ryne Sandberg—Whenever the Cubs were on a hot streak, Ryno would eat the same meals at the same restaurants. He would also leave for the ballpark at the same time each day.

Turk Wendell—One of the most superstitious players ever, he would chew four pieces of black licorice when he pitched, brush his teeth between innings, kangaroo-hop over the baselines, and squat on the mound whenever his catcher stood.

Greg Maddux—Ate blueberry pancakes on the mornings of his starts.

Moises Alou—Urinated on his hands to toughen them up.

Mark DeRosa—Whenever he goes hitless, he changes his batting gloves and bat for the next game.

HANDY ANDY'S BIG BLUNDER

Cubs All-Star outfielder Andy Pafko made one well-remembered gaffe. In a 1949 game against the St. Louis Cardinals, Pafko claimed he caught a bloop fly off the bat of Rocky Nelson. However, umpire Al Barlick ruled that Pafko had trapped the ball. Pafko argued but never called time out, so Nelson kept running to complete what **became humorously known as baseball's only "inside-the-glove" home run.**

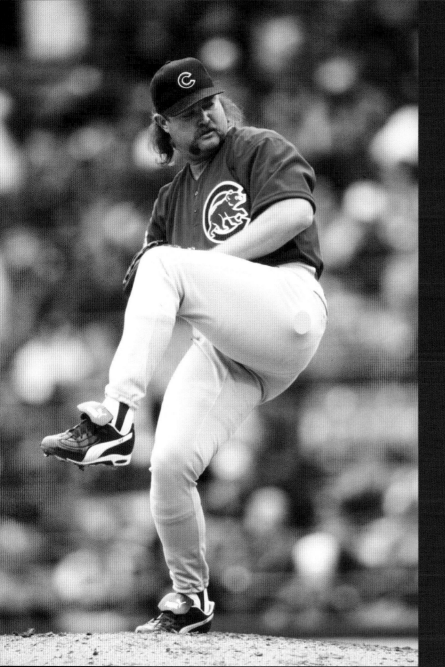

> ## "It's a role where you have to be a cool customer. You have to go out there and let it all hang out for an inning."

—Cubs general manager Jim Hendry
ON THE MINDSET OF A BULLPEN CLOSER

Rod Beck was the Cubs star closer in 1998 with 51 saves.

A TIP OF THE CAP TO CAP ANSON

Brawny, powerful, and iron-willed, Cap Anson was pro baseball's first true superstar and perhaps **the best player of the 19th century.** He was also one of the greatest and most influential players in Cubs history. Combining power and smarts both on and off the field, Adrian Constantine Anson was a stalwart on the team for 22 seasons (player-manager for 19 of them).

After debuting with the Philadelphia Athletics of the National Association in 1871, the powerful right-hander joined the White Stockings in '76. As player-manager, "Cap" settled himself in at first base and dug in at the plate as well, collecting two batting titles, 2,076 RBI, and 3,418 hits (the first big-leaguer to reach 3,000), and racking up a lifetime batting average of .333.

As a manager, Anson was innovative and aggressive, leading his team to five NL championships and 1,283 victories (both remain team records). His .578 winning percentage is among the all-time best. He was **among the first to implement the hit-and-run, utilize a pitching rotation, and use a third base coach.** He also introduced the sport to the concept of spring training.

Anson was very popular among fans, teammates, and opponents; however, he was also an open racist who refused to let his team compete against teams that fielded black players. In fact, his actions played a large part in keeping baseball closed to African Americans for more than a half century.

In 1897, the hard-nosed, 45-year-old future Hall of Famer capped off a 27-year career by slugging two homers on his final afternoon in the majors, at a time when other ballplayers were watching their careers fizzle out around age 30.

After 22 years with the White Stockings, Anson was so strongly identified with the team that after he left the club, they were known for several years as "The Orphans."

RIGGS STEPHENSON

His nickname was "Old Hoss," and Riggs Stephenson's reliability at the plate was as solid as an old barnyard animal. With a lifetime batting average of .336, the 14-year major leaguer was **probably the least heralded great hitter in Cubs history.**

A shoulder injury suffered while playing football at the University of Alabama limited some of Stephenson's throwing ability. But when he suited up as a member of the Cubs from 1926 to 1934, some said that **the trio of Hack Wilson, Kiki Cuyler, and Stephenson was the best outfield of all time.**

Stephenson was neither flamboyant nor a slugger, and perhaps that lack of color in his game has prevented him from getting his due and (despite his lifetime average) has kept him out of the Hall of Fame.

MAJOR LEAGUE TOTALS			
G	**HR**	**RBI**	**BA**
1,310	63	773	.336

Sammy Sosa

was the first player to hit a home run against every active MLB team—including the Cubs. He was also the first player in major-league history to hit more than 60 home runs in a season three times in his career. He smacked 66 in 1998, 63 in '99, and 64 in 2001.

GETTING CLOSER TO THE PRIZE

When Lou Piniella was named the Cubs' new skipper for the 2007 season, he announced that he'd come to Chicago to win a championship.

Cubs fans liked the sound of that—and they liked what they saw in Piniella: a proven track record with the Reds, Yanks, and Mariners, and a World Series title on his résumé. His reputation as a field boss with a short fuse was of little consequence compared to his winning attitude.

Piniella insisted that he had mellowed, but as the season began, fans waited for the new skipper to blow up. Despite the Cubs kicking off the season in lackluster fashion, it took the feisty manager more than a month to put on a show. The explosion came on June 2, when, in the course of an argument with the third-base umpire, an outraged **Piniella lost his temper and kicked dirt onto the ump.** He was

tossed from the game, and it seemed as if someone flipped a switch. Up to that point, the Cubs were 22–30, had lost 5 games in a row, and were 7½ games out of first. After that, the players and the fans seemed revived. And just like that, the Cubs started winning.

It may have been the spark the team needed, but talent was more likely the reason for the improvement. The Tribune Company had loosened the purse strings to an

unprecedented level during the off-season, investing $300 million in long-term contracts. The investment was beginning to pay dividends.

Among the most conspicuous "gets" they ponied up for were pitcher Ted Lilly, the versatile Mark DeRosa, and outfielder Alfonso Soriano, who signed a long-term, break-the-bank deal worth $136 million. For once the Cubs seemed to be going for broke.

The high-profile newcomers jelled with the veteran Cubs, and together the team made it happen, notching 85 victories in the regular season—a 19-game improvement over 2006. Top players Aramis Ramirez, Derrek Lee, and Carlos Zambrano had first-rate seasons. Soriano, who hit 33 home runs and drove in 70, was a spark plug. And in the stretch, management called up some young players from the farm, notably catcher Geovany Soto, who hit .389 in 24 games and provided some late-season flair.

The Cubs gritted it out to finish the season at 85–77, two games over Milwaukee, and the fans were positively giddy. Bring on the Diamondbacks! Cubs fans couldn't help but get ahead of themselves, with visions of the World Series floating in their heads. But then they were once again slammed back into gruesome reality as they watched their beloved Cubs get swept by Arizona. Once again, Cubs fans were left with their hearts broken and the words "Wait 'til next year" ringing in their ears. Yes, it was going to be at least a full 100 years of rebuilding since the last Series crown.

After the postseason letdown, general manager Jim Hendry perked up the hopes of Cubs Nation by again demonstrating a "win now" mentality. Once again the checkbook came out, and the Cubs won a bidding war for Japanese transplant Kosuke Fukudome.

With Piniella and most of the '07 team returning for '08, it seemed all the pieces were in place to become the first Cubs team in a century to reach the playoffs in back-to-back years and this time, finally win that ever-elusive World Series title.

LEE ELIA'S RANT

The Cubs were not playing well in 1983, and the spectators that came out to Wrigley Field booed to remind them. On April 29, Cubs manager Lee Elia snapped after a 4–3 loss to the Dodgers before 9,391 fans, saying, among other things:

". . .Eighty-five percent of the world is working, but the 15 percent who come out to Wrigley Field have nothing better to do than heap abuse and criticism on the team. Why don't they go out and look for jobs?"

That was the highlight of Elia's rant, which **ran 4½ minutes and contained 46 profanities among 448 words.** The tape of his meltdown was played all over the country, and Elia was not the manager of the Cubs for much longer. He was fired in August.

"Never in my wildest dreams did I think someone would run out of there and put it on the air."

—LEE ELIA

Notable "Take Me Out to the Ball Game" Singers Since Harry Caray Died in 1998

- Widow Dutchie Caray

- Legendary Cubs third baseman and current broadcaster Ron Santo

- Former Bears coach Mike Ditka

- Actor John Cusack

- Pearl Jam lead singer Eddie Vedder

- Barney the Dinosaur

- Actor Jeremy Piven

- Race-car driver Jeff Gordon

- Blackhawks player Patrick Kane

- Singer Ozzy Osbourne

- Cubs broadcaster Pat Hughes

- Hall of Fame second baseman Ryne Sandberg

- Disc jockey Dick Biondi

- Broadcaster Chip Caray

- Smashing Pumpkins lead singer Billy Corgan

HOME RUN CHASE
BALLHAWKS OUTSIDE WRIGLEY FIELD

One way some fans choose to have fun at the ballpark is just being near the park—outside the fences. On any given day that the Cubs are playing at home, dozens of fans gather outside Wrigley Field—especially on Waveland Avenue—and position themselves in the street or on the sidewalk, ready to snatch home run balls as they come soaring over the outfield wall. During the home run showdown between Mark McGwire and Sammy Sosa in 1998 and the 2003 National League playoffs, hundreds of people gathered outside the park, and police crowd control was needed.

In general, **ballhawks are fans who cannot afford or cannot obtain tickets to watch the game inside the park** or would simply rather compete for baseballs than watch the game. A certain nimbleness is required to succeed at this endeavor. Just like an outfielder, **a ballhawk must be quick to respond to the crack of the bat,** trying to guess where the ball will land, then must dash to the spot and often use elbows to fight off others with the same plan.

In the end, the winner of the ball sweepstakes is either the possessor of a nifty souvenir or (given the current climate in the memorabilia world) has acquired an item he can sell on eBay. Knowing this, it's safe to say that a home run hit by the opposing team that comes soaring back onto the playing field is not the actual home run ball, but a decoy launched to appease the fans inside the stadium and fulfill the "Throw it back" tradition.

THE CUBS CONVENTION

The brainchild of former Cubs marketing director John McDonough, the off-season Cubs Convention has paid dividends thousands of times over since its inception in 1986.

Each January, over a three-day weekend at a downtown Chicago hotel, Cubs officials, coaches, and players past and present mingle with fans, sign autographs, chat about seasons past, and discuss hopes for the coming season. There is also a "state of the union" address from the general manager. Because it is usually rare to have the opportunity to shake hands with a player, it is the personal touch that goes so far, giving fans the chance to get up close and personal with their heroes.

More than 20,000 fans attended the 23rd annual Cubs Convention in 2008—and each year tickets sell out months in advance. The idea has been so popular that other major-league teams have emulated the convention with dramatic success. And when the Chicago Blackhawks hockey team announced their first off-season convention would be held in July 2008, it sold out almost immediately.

Manager Dusty Baker and his son Darren at the 2003 Cubs Convention

LIVE MUSIC AT THE FRIENDLY CONFINES

In recent years, the longtime baseball tradition of using organ players to entertain fans and play "Take Me Out to the Ball Game" during the seventh-inning stretch has been eroding. One by one, teams have been eliminating the use of live organ players in favor of recorded music before, during, and after games, as well as during the stretch.

By 2008, live organ music remained in use at only about one-third of major-league parks. This phase-out has not occurred at Wrigley Field, where Gary Pressy has been playing live at home games since 1987 and is still going strong. He plays "I Walk the Line" whenever a batter takes a base on balls and once played "You're Sixteen (You're Beautiful and You're Mine)" as a game entered the 16th inning.

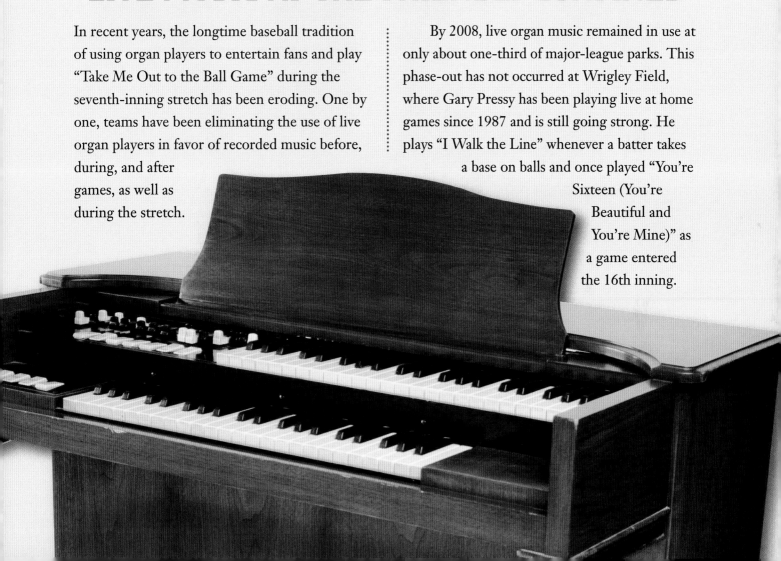

CRUSHING ROCKS

On August 18, 1995, the Cubs defeated the Colorado Rockies 26–7 in Denver, where the air was thinner than in Chicago, and it didn't matter if the wind was blowing in or out. Luis Gonzalez drove in six runs as the Cubs clouted the Rockies. As an added insult to the Rockies, there was a 2-hour, 45-minute rain delay. The run total equaled the Cubs' high-water mark and tied the post-1900 major-league record, which was broken in 2007 when the Texas Rangers scored 30 runs against the Baltimore Orioles.

SPRING TRAINING IN THE DESERT

Historic ballpark. Toughest ticket in town. Packed stands full of fun-loving fans. If it feels a lot like a summer game at Wrigley Field, that's just the way the folks in Mesa, Arizona, like it.

The Cubs are the hottest show in the Cactus League each spring, when **Hohokam Park** buzzes with the anticipation that maybe—just maybe—this will be the Cubs' year. The stadium is one of the largest in spring training baseball, holding more than 12,000 fans. That, and the Cubs' loyal following, has allowed the club to set Cactus League attendance records.

Why not spend a March afternoon there? The venue offers close proximity for autograph seekers, a giant video screen on the left-field scoreboard, and grass seating in the outfield with views of snowcapped mountains in the distance. The dimensions of the park match those of Wrigley Field.

"Hohokam" is a Native American phrase meaning "those who vanished." The Cubs arrived in 1952 and vanished briefly to Long Beach, California, in 1966 and to Scottsdale, Arizona, in the 1960s and '70s. Since their return in '79, Mesa has been a spring training mecca for Cubs fans everywhere.

BROADCAST BANTER
THE PAT AND RON SHOW

Play-by-play man Pat Hughes is not easily flustered by anything that happens on the field or in the booth and maintains his poise at all times. That demeanor, coupled with the velvet in his voice, makes Hughes a consummate professional when it comes to sportscasters. He would have to be, given that he spent 12 years with humorist Bob Uecker in the Milwaukee Brewers' booth and has shared the Cubs' WGN microphone with say-anything Ron Santo since 1996.

Santo, revered former third baseman for the Cubs, is the off-the-cuff color man. Hughes TELLS FANS WHAT HAPPENED. Santo REACTS TO WHAT HAPPENS, whether it is with a groan or a whoop. Strange things can happen in a broadcast booth—like the time Santo singed his toupee on the overhead heaters at Shea Stadium during a game in April 2003. Santo shouted and fanned the smoke but quickly returned to his announcing role.

Santo and Hughes have such a comical camaraderie and banter going during games that even when the Cubs are getting clobbered, many fans stay tuned in to chuckle at their repartee. A large number of **fans even admit to muting the sound on their televisions to listen to Pat and Ron while watching the games**—even if there is a several-second delay, which can trick unsuspecting listeners into thinking that Hughes is psychic and can predict the next play.

Ron Santo and Pat Hughes

"FRIENDLY" FACTS ABOUT THE "CONFINES"

• Wrigley Field's capacity is 41,160, among the smallest in the majors, yet the Cubs consistently rank among the top 10 in major-league attendance.

• Built in 1914, Wrigley Field is the second-oldest major-league stadium after Boston's Fenway Park.

- The park is built on grounds that used to house a Lutheran seminary.

- Wrigley Field was originally called Weeghman Park (1914–19) and was also called Cubs Park (1920–25).

- A batted baseball has never hit the center-field scoreboard, but shots hit by Roberto Clemente (1959) and Bill Nicholson (1948) came close. However, golf pro Sam Snead once teed off from home plate and drove a golf ball onto the legendary scoreboard.

- The left-field foul pole bears flags with No. 14 (Ernie Banks) and No. 10 (Ron Santo). The right-field pole honors No. 26 (Billy Williams) and No. 23 (Ryne Sandberg).

- Wrigley Field hosted the 1947, 1962, and 1990 All-Star Games.

- The largest crowd ever to watch a Cubs game at Wrigley Field was 51,556 on June 27, 1930.

However, paid attendance for that game against the Brooklyn Dodgers was less than 20,000, due to a Ladies' Day promotion that let most patrons in for free.

- The grass field at Wrigley is a blend of Kentucky bluegrass and rye.

- Fans in the bleachers—and even those on the streets beyond them—routinely throw opposing home run balls back onto the field, while keeping ones hit by the home team.

- The Cubs played their first night game at Wrigley Field on August 8, 1988. It was rained out after 3½ innings, so the first *official* night game took place the following night as the Cubs edged the Mets 6–4. However, this was not the first night game played at Wrigley Field. In July 1943, the All-American Girls Professional Baseball League held their All-Star Game at the Friendly Confines using temporary lighting structures.

CUBS QUIZ

1. What team did the Cubs beat in the 1908 World Series?

. . . .

2. Which former Cubs catcher was once traded for himself?

. . . .

3. Where did 2008 Cubs infielders **Ryan Theriot** and **Mike Fontenot** previously star together?

. . . .

4. What is the nickname of the Cubs' Single-A minor-league affiliate in Boise, Idaho?

5. Did Ernie Banks play in more games for the Cubs, or did he have more hits?

6. Who is **Ryne Sandberg** named after?

1. The Detroit Tigers, four games to one; 2. Harry Chiti was purchased by the Mets from Cleveland in April 1962 for a player to be named later. Two months later he was sent back to Cleveland as that player; 3. They made up the middle infield for Louisiana State's 2000 College World Series championship team; 4. The Hawks; 5. More hits—2,583 to 2,528 games played; 6. Ryne Duren—a three-time All-Star, journeyman relief pitcher (most notably with the Yankees in the late 1950s/early 1960s) known for his blazing fastball and thick glasses.

CHAPTER FIVE

"THE CUBBIES ARE ROCKIN'"

"The Cubbies are rockin' all over town.

There's a new sensation, and it's really comin' down.

North side of Chicago, Waveland Avenue,

There's magic in the air, a new point of view."

—WORDS AND MUSIC BY BARRY GOLDBERG AND ARAM GOLDBERG, 1989

Aramis Ramirez watches his home run ball soar into the bleachers.

"Once a Cub, always a Cub."

—Ernie Banks

MAKING MUSIC IN '84

In the heat of the pennant race during the '84 season, several Cubs players recorded a song called "Men in Blue." Written by James Ritz and Allen Petrowski, **THE TOE-TAPPING COUNTRY TUNE** sung by Jody Davis, Rick Sutcliffe, Leon Durham, Keith Moreland, and Gary Woods never won a Grammy, but **it remains one of the most popular songs in Cubs Nation.** With a catchy melody and lyrics like "It's been a long, long time since 1945, but the Wrigley faithful have always kept the spirit alive," the song still inspires the Cubs and their loyal fans to "keep 'em flying high for Cubbie blue."

SLAMMIN' SAMMY SOSA

MAJOR LEAGUE TOTALS			
G	HR	RBI	BA
2,354	609	1,667	.273

Cubs fans owe thanks to the White Sox for this one. And they should also tip their caps to the Texas Rangers, whose then-team president (a guy named George W. Bush) conceded that allowing Sosa to slip away was the biggest mistake he made with the Rangers. Their loss was the Cubs' gain when they welcomed Slammin' Sammy Sosa to the North Side in 1992.

Born into poverty in the Dominican Republic, Sosa was determined to make it big in baseball. He had plenty of raw talent, but when he didn't progress quickly enough for the Rangers and the Sox, both teams let him go. Sosa made them both regret it. By 1995, when he started cranking home runs at a rate of 35 to 40 per season and driving in more than 100 runs per year, Wrigley Field was awash in a sea of Sosa jerseys. Soon Sosa was a superstar, living large and soaking up the love and applause directed his way. Listed at a powerful 6'0" and 190 pounds, the once poor, skinny kid had grown up to strike fear in pitchers around the major leagues.

Fans were as attracted to his infectious smile and good nature as they were to his wicked bat. His quirks were endearing to many—the little hop in the batter's box when he believed he'd hit a home run and the love tap directed at his cheering fans as he ran out to right field at full sprint.

But Sosa's popularity was never greater than in 1998, as he pummeled the ball at a phenomenal rate, collecting 158 RBI on his way to an incredible 66 home runs. As Sosa and Cardinals slugger Mark McGwire chased Roger Maris's single-season record of 61 homers, they were both thrust into the spotlight, where the exuberant Sosa shined on the national stage. In the end, McGwire got to 62 first, and when he hit the milestone dinger on September 8 against the Cubs, Sammy applauded him louder than anybody. Sosa finished the season with 66 long balls (to McGwire's 70), and he also walked away with league MVP honors and a trip to the playoffs.

Slammin' Sammy was on top of the world. He smashed his 500th career home run in 2003. The seven-time All-Star said he believed the more home runs he hit, the more everyone would love him, and indeed they did.

Alas, the love didn't last. In 2004, Sosa spent time on the DL for back spasms caused by a violent sneeze. He slumped badly upon his return, although his ego and unreliability swelled more than ever. At the end of the season, amidst friction between Sosa and his teammates, his manager Dusty Baker, and his loyal fan base, Sammy was last seen arriving late and departing early from the final game of the season—without authorization. During the off-season, after 13 years with the club and a team-record 545 home runs in a Cubs uniform, he was traded to the Baltimore Orioles.

In the years since Sosa's departure from the Cubs, his reputation has taken more than a few hits, but one need only look at his career stats and the records he set to appreciate the full impact he had on the Cubs' franchise.

RYNO'S RARE ERROR

Months after first baseman Leon Durham watched a ground ball slip between his legs during the 1984 National League Championship Series helping San Diego rally to defeat the Cubs, it was revealed that Ryne Sandberg had accidentally knocked over a cooler of Gatorade that soaked Durham's mitt. Towels and a hand dryer were employed to dry it after coach Don Zimmer told Durham, "I think you should go ahead and use that glove anyway, Bull. It might bring you good luck."

> ## "I've only been doing this 54 years. With a little experience, I might get better."
>
> —Harry Caray, near the end of his
> broadcasting career

CELEBRITY CUBS FANS

- Comedian Tom Dreesen

- Actor **Bill Murray**

- Actor John Cusack

- Comedian Jeff Garlin

- Actor Jim Belushi

- Actor **Bonnie Hunt**

- Actor Dennis Franz

- Actor Vince Vaughn

- Singer **Billy Corgan** of the Smashing Pumpkins

- U.S. Senator Hillary Clinton

- Actor **William Peterson**

- Singer Eddie Vedder of Pearl Jam

- Actor **Gary Sinise**

- Comedian George Wendt

WILL WORK FOR TIPS

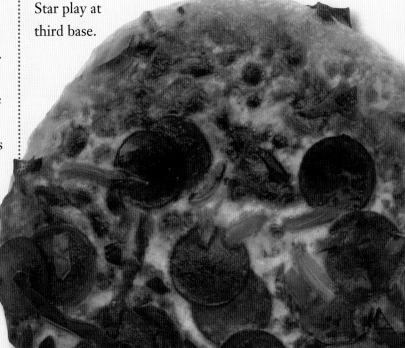

Longtime Cubs fans generally agree that Ron Santo deserves a spot in the Baseball Hall of Fame. Those who ordered from his pizza joint on a particular Saturday in the early 1960s can tell you how well-rounded the star third baseman is.

You see, Santo got a call saying a Santo's Pizza deliveryman was out sick on a hectic night. Instead of trying to find a replacement driver, Ron went to the pizzeria in Park Ridge, a suburb of Chicago, and started delivering orders himself.

"Here I was, a major league third baseman, making pizza deliveries in my Cadillac," he wrote in his autobiography, *Ron Santo: For Love of Ivy*, "but I knew it was essential to keep the customers happy and loyal."

Actually, one customer followed a stern complaint about a late delivery with a special request. He wanted to know if the deliveryman could have Santo autograph a baseball for his son. It took some doing, but Santo eventually convinced the man that he was, indeed, Ron Santo, and that he could handle that request on the spot.

Santo opened six other locations and saw Santo's Pizza slices served at Wrigley Field, where the only thing he had to worry about delivering was All-Star play at third base.

"JOLLY CHOLLY": CHARLIE GRIMM

Player, manager, broadcaster, and front office executive for more than 40 years, Charlie Grimm did it all for the Cubs. He was a sturdy, excellent first baseman for two decades (he led the National League in fielding percentage nine times) and three different times served as manager of the team. Whenever owner P. K. Wrigley felt his club needed shaking up, he brought back Grimm to get a handle on the team.

The cheerful, popular Grimm loved the Cubs and delivered solid leadership. When Wrigley tired of Rogers Hornsby's autocratic ways and fired him during the 1932 season, he tapped Grimm, still an active player at that point, to replace him. With **an affable, fun-loving personality that earned him the nickname "Jolly Cholly"** and endeared him to players and fans, Grimm couldn't have been more different than Hornsby. Grimm's presence also translated into victories, as the team claimed three pennants under

his command. The first came in 1932, his first season at the helm. When Grimm took over the team on August 2, they were in second place with a 53–46 record. Under Grimm, they wrapped up the season with 37 wins and 18 losses to win the pennant. In 1935, Grimm led the team to a 100-win season and another pennant.

Grimm was relieved of his job during the 1938 season (most reports claim he voluntarily resigned), and the team flourished without him. It helped that new manager Gabby Hartnett had player Gabby Hartnett at the plate to smack a pennant-clinching home run (the famous Homer in the Gloamin'). Meanwhile, Grimm, still a favorite of owner P. K. Wrigley, remained with the club as a broadcaster. He departed for a short time to manage the Cubs' top farm team (Milwaukee), but in 1944, he returned to Chicago when he was once again handed the Cubs' managerial reins. Fans and players welcomed him back, especially after a dismal start to the season and a particularly ugly nine-game losing streak under previous manager Jimmie Wilson. In 1945, just the second year in his second tour as Cubs manager, Grimm led the Cubs to the third World Series of his tenure.

As the team rounded out the 1940s with a pair of last-place finishes, Grimm was removed from the clubhouse once again. This time he was named director of player personnel before he left for a series of managerial positions. The Cubs came calling again in 1960. At age 61, the still-beloved Grimm returned to the team for his third stint as field boss. But just 17 games into the season, and with the Cubs off to a 6–11 start, P. K. Wrigley decided his broadcaster, Lou Boudreau (former All-Star and player-manager for the Cleveland Indians), would be better off in the dugout and Grimm would be better off behind the microphone. Wrigley turned to broadcaster Jack Brickhouse to broker the deal without hurting too many feelings, and Boudreau and Grimm swapped jobs for the rest of the season.

"A manager for a broadcaster," Brickhouse lamented. "Only with the Cubs."

MAJOR LEAGUE TOTALS			
G	HR	RBI	BA
2,166	79	1,078	.290

KILLER K'S
KERRY WOOD'S 20 STRIKEOUT GAME

At the start of the 1998 season, Cubs rookie Kerry Wood had the fans all abuzz. Wood appeared to be the linear descendent of Nolan Ryan and Roger Clemens, the next in a series of great Texas power pitchers who could anchor a pitching rotation.

Early in the '98 season, in an awe-inspiring game that seemed to be a promise fulfilled, Wood wrote the type of history that fans never forget. On May 6 at Wrigley Field, Wood overpowered Houston with a stunning performance, shutting out the Astros on one hit, walking none, and striking out 20 batters—a show of dominance that tied the MLB single-game strikeout record, (set by Wood's hero, Roger Clemens).

It was a warm, overcast afternoon, and there were just 15,758 fans on hand. Twenty-year-old Wood did not make the Cubs roster out of spring training because the club was afraid to rush him, but much admiration of his fastball (which touched 100 miles per hour twice during the record-setting game) was voiced. Wood made one start with the Iowa Cubs (AAA) before he got the call to Chicago.

Before the Houston game, Wood was just 2–2 in his first four starts, with an inflated 5.89 earned run average. Like Chicago's weather, he could be hot and cold on the same day.

"I had no idea how many [strikeouts] I had going into the last three innings. After the first inning, I knew I had three, and I lost track after that.... I wasn't really worried about the strikeouts.... It just felt like I was playing catch."

—KERRY WOOD

Since they drafted him in 1995, the Cubs had been waiting on Wood's fastball. They knew they had a special player but had no idea that his arrival in the majors would be announced with fireworks.

On this fateful day, Wood recorded 11 strikeouts through five innings, striking out the side in the first and the fifth. Only two Astros reached base that day: Wood surrendered a single to Ricky Gutierrez in the third and hit Craig Biggio with a pitch in the sixth.

In fact, Wood actually seemed to gain momentum as the game advanced, striking out seven straight Astros between the seventh and ninth innings. Fittingly, the game's last out was also a K.

When the game ended in a 2–0 shutout, Wood was mobbed on the mound by his teammates. He had no idea how many Astros had gone down on strikes. A broadcaster finally told him it was 20 and that he'd tied Clemens's major-league record for strikeouts in a game, set a new National League record for strikeouts in a game, and set the new Cubs' team record.

KEN HUBBS

Young, friendly, and talented, Ken Hubbs was a budding star, who looked like he would hold down the Cubs' second-base job for a decade. The NL's Rookie of the Year in 1962 went 78 consecutive games and 418 chances without an error. In fact, he was so slick around the bag that he was **the first rookie ever to win a Gold Glove Award.** Hubbs again turned in a solid performance in '63, leaving Cubs management confident in their young second-sacker.

According to his roommate Ron Santo, Hubbs had a fear of flying. But the young man took flying lessons to overcome his fear, and during spring training in 1964, he surprised Santo by showing him the pilot's license he had earned just two weeks earlier. **But then tragedy struck on February 13, when the single-engine Cessna plane Hubbs was piloting crashed** on a frozen lake in Utah, killing him and his passenger. It was an unimaginable loss for his family and an immeasurable one for the Cubs as well. Santo, Ernie Banks, and four other Cubs served as pallbearers at the funeral of their beloved and much-respected teammate.

NEW KID ON THE BLOCK

The loss of Ken Hubbs in an airplane accident left a gaping hole in the Cubs' infield. They struggled through the 1964 season, but then another terrific rookie came along to claim the position in 1965. But Glenn Beckert was so naive as a young player that he once tried to run through (instead of around) a screen set up near the bases during infield practice to protect fielders from errant throws. Nevertheless, Beckert out-fought all other candidates to start 154 games that season, and he went on to post a .283 lifetime batting average in his 11 major-league seasons.

2008
BREAKING RECORDS AND REACHING MILESTONES

The Cubs enjoyed a banner 2008 season, accomplishing several feats no other Cubs team in history had managed and several others that had not been done since magical seasons of long ago. The following is a list of some of their top '08 feats.

The Cubs...

- Entered June with the best record in baseball for the first time since 1908.

- Reached three million Wrigley Field fans faster than any team in franchise history (in the 74th home game on September 2).

- Set a new single-season attendance record with 3,300,200 fans visiting Wrigley Field—the highest in the history of Chicago sports.

- Tied a National League record by having eight players chosen for the All-Star Game, including an unprecedented two rookies in the starting lineup.

- Played the White Sox while both teams were in first place for the first time in 11 seasons of interleague play. The last time the two teams battled while in first place was during the 1906 World Series.

- Swept the season series with the Atlanta Braves for the first time since the rivalry between the two franchises began in 1876.

- Won nine straight games on the road in July and August—their longest road winning streak since taking 12 in a row in 1945.

- Won 97 games—the most since 1945.

- Moved 30 games over .500 for the first time since their 1984 team finished the season 96–65.

- Won the 10,000th game in franchise history, following the Giants to become just the second franchise in the majors to reach the milestone.

- Won 55 games at home—the most since the 1935 Cubs.

- Won 14 straight home games—the most since 1936.

- Beginning with a sweep of the Brewers in late July, the Cubs won nine straight series (of two or more games) for the first time since they won ten series in a row in 1907.

- Reached the playoffs for the second straight year, the first time the Cubs had done so since 1907 and 1908.

- Moved into first place on May 11 and stayed there for the rest of the season (151 days)—the longest stretch since 1969.

HIPPO VAUGHN

In what was perhaps the greatest two-sided pitching masterpiece in major-league history, Cubs pitcher Hippo Vaughn **threw 9⅓ hitless innings and lost.**

On May 2, 1917, Vaughn, in the prime of his 13-year major-league career, faced off against Cincinnati's Fred Toney in a remarkable game. **Both pitchers cruised through nine innings without surrendering a hit,** but with one out in the top of the tenth at Weeghman Park (later known as Wrigley Field), Vaughn gave up a single to Reds shortstop Larry Kopf, thus terminating his no-hitter.

Two batters later a hitter reached on an error. A short chopper in front of the plate eventually brought in the game's only run with Vaughn frantically trying to field the ball and his catcher dropping the throw. Toney completed his ten-inning no-hitter, and the Cubs fell 1–0.

"KING" KELLY

The ballplayer born Michael Joseph Kelly was crowned "King" by baseball fans who loved his flashy style and his speed, skill, and blatant disregard for the rules—both on and off the field.

Kelly joined the Chicago White Stockings in 1880 and took the city by storm. En route to five NL titles, he twice won the league's batting title (in 1884 and '86) and topped the circuit in runs scored for three consecutive years (1884–86). The flamboyant catcher-outfielder was without doubt the most exciting player in the sport, due in part to his powerful bat (he hit over .300 eight times) and daring baserunning maneuvers. One of his favorite tricks was to cut corners on the basepaths when the ump wasn't looking, running directly from first to third or second to home—whichever he could get away with. He is credited with perfecting the takeout slide at second to break up double plays and, on defense, was known to trip base-runners and hide extra balls in the grass for when he needed them.

The handsome and charismatic Kelly loved the limelight, and the fans loved him. He lived according to his own rules, carousing late into the night, drinking, and generally living it up. Although he remained wildly popular on and off the field, teetotaler White Stockings owner Al Spalding grew tired of his antics and sold him to the Boston Braves after the 1886 championship season for the then-unheard-of sum of $10,000. Chicago fans were furious, but Boston welcomed him as—what else—a king.

SET IN STONE—OR BRONZE

On a rainy Opening Day, March 31, 2008, the Cubs unveiled a bronze statue of Mr. Cub, Ernie Banks, outside of Wrigley Field. Banks's likeness joined the statue of late broadcaster Harry Caray as one of two the team has erected to honor its long heritage as one of the first teams in the National League.

"This should have happened 10 or 15 years ago. [Banks was] the greatest ambassador for baseball, and still is a great ambassador for baseball."

—HANK AARON

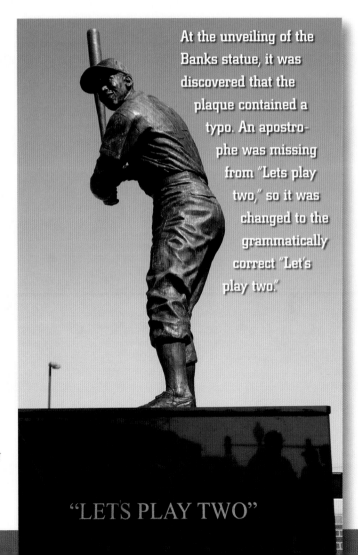

At the unveiling of the Banks statue, it was discovered that the plaque contained a typo. An apostrophe was missing from "Lets play two," so it was changed to the grammatically correct "Let's play two."

"LET'S PLAY TWO"

WRIGLEY FAMILY

Chewing gum magnate William Wrigley, Jr., found a fresh product to chew on in late 1918: the Chicago Cubs. As owner Charlie Weeghman began selling off his shares of the team, minority investor Wrigley snapped them up.

Wrigley, a Philadelphia native, had broken off from his family's soap manufacturing busi-ness in the early 1890s and moved to Chicago, where he began writing his own success story. By 1893, with the introduction of Juicy Fruit and Wrigley's Spearmint gum, he was among the wealthiest businessmen in Chicago and was one of nine investors rounded up by Weeghman to purchase the Cubs in January 1916. By 1920, Wrigley was the majority owner of the team; in 1926, he changed the name of the ballpark to Wrigley Field.

Determined to achieve the success and popularity the club had once enjoyed, the chewing gum magnate poured money rather freely into the franchise. Though he never won the world championship he sought as Cubs owner, he remained committed to building a competitive team. He appointed Bill Veeck, Sr., as president, and together with manager Joe McCarthy the trio built a powerhouse club. Wrigley remained at the helm of the team until his death in 1932,

Grover Alexander, William Wrigley, and Bill Killefer

when ownership passed into the hands of his son, 37-year-old Philip Knight (P. K.) Wrigley.

P. K. had a different style of stewardship. While the club did win three league titles in his first seven years as owner, P. K. didn't love baseball like his father had. For one thing, he was more conservative with his checkbook, choosing to put more money and attention into sprucing up the ballpark to maximize profits rather than improve the roster. He had no interest in being the club's president and, in fact, only grudgingly stepped in to fill the position a year after Bill Veeck's death in 1933. P. K. Wrigley held the post until his own death in 1977, keeping the Cubs and Wrigley Field in the city's heart through good times and bad—despite seldom attending games himself.

P. K. Wrigley, his wife Helen, and son William

Upon his death, his only son, William III, inherited the franchise—the third generation of Wrigley family ownership. For 65 years the Wrigley family had been synonymous with the team, but in 1981, William sold the franchise to The Tribune Company for $20.5 million.

During World War II, with most able-bodied men serving in the armed forces, P. K. Wrigley started the All-American Girls Professional Baseball League (AAGPBL), which the movie *A League of Their Own* was based upon.

MARK DeROSA:
MR. VERSATILITY

As the Cubs' resident blogger, Mark DeRosa is usually right in the middle of the action in the clubhouse. He conducts interviews for his MLB blog, "The Pulse," talks fantasy football, chats up reporters, and keeps teammates on their toes.

Center stage has become a comfortable place for DeRosa on the field as well.

Once considered a valuable utility player, DeRosa emerged in 2008 as a bona fide star. Even though his home is at the second sack, he has played every infield position in his two seasons with the Cubs and serves regular stints at the corner outfield spots. And in '08 he stepped up his offense as well, shattering his previous career bests in home runs, RBI, runs, stolen bases, and walks, among other categories.

In August, DeRosa became the first Cubs player since Fred McGriff in 2001 to go deep in four consecutive games. This from a man who, before 2008, had never launched more than 13 home runs in a season.

"I can't explain them, to be honest with you," DeRosa told reporters with a smile, perhaps saving the actual explanation for his blog. "I don't know. I'm getting pitches to drive, and I'm not missing them."

DeRosa rarely misses a chance to poke friendly fun at a teammate, a dynamic that seems to keep the Cubs' clubhouse relaxed and lighthearted. For example, while interviewing rookie pitcher Jeff Samardzija, DeRosa pointed out that he's able to have quiet dinners out on the town because he's married with a child, unlike Samardzija—a single guy "with long, flowing locks who was an All-America [football player] at Notre Dame."

But if he keeps improving on his prowess at the plate, DeRosa might soon find his own uninterrupted dinners hard to come by.

CUBS NICKNAMES

- The Hawk—Andre Dawson

- The Duke of Tralee—**Roger Bresnahan**

- Bull—Leon Durham

- High Pockets—George Kelly

- The Gravedigger—Richie Hebner

- Popeye—**Don Zimmer**

- The Lip—Leo Durocher

- The Old Fox—Clark Griffith

- Jolly Cholly—Charlie Grimm

- Mad Dog—Greg Maddux and Bill Madlock

- Sweet-Swinging Billy—**Billy Williams**

- Parson—Billy Sunday

"For seven months, we've been hearing about 1969 and the wind and the sun and the ivy and the moon. But it's over. . . . No more monkey on our backs!!"

—CUBS MANAGER JIM FREY, WHEN THE TEAM ADVANCED TO POSTSEASON PLAY IN 1984 FOR THE FIRST TIME IN 39 YEARS

GABBY HARTNETT

Without doubt, the "Homer in the Gloamin'" is one of the defining moments in Cubs history. But even without it, Charles Leo "Gabby" Hartnett would have gone down in the books as one of the Cubs' all-time greats.

A superb catcher who also hit for power and a high average, Hartnett spent all but one of his 20 major-league seasons with the Cubs (1922–40), also managing the team for the last three. One of the best catchers in the game through the first half of the 20th century, he racked up **a lifetime .297 batting average, powered 236 home runs, and was the 1935 NL MVP.** So, where'd the nickname come from? Hartnett proved to be most chatty with umpires and opponents while perched behind the plate.

For all his excellence behind the plate and in front of it, Hartnett's name will forever be linked to one event. And what an event it was! On September 28, 1938, the Cubs were battling the league-leading Pittsburgh Pirates for first place. As dusk fell on Wrigley Field, the score was tied at five apiece in the bottom of the ninth, and plate umpire George Barr had already declared the game would be called after that frame. Hartnett came to the plate with two outs, and, at precisely 5:37 P.M., he jacked Mace Brown's two-strike curve into the darkening shadows of Wrigley Field's brand-new left-field bleachers. **Delirious fans mobbed the field, celebrating the Cubs' victory as Gabby rounded the bases.** The home run that was clouted in such dramatic fashion also proved to be the difference-maker in the season; the Hartnett-managed squad took the lead after that game and rode it all the way to the World Series.

Hartnett's bat and catcher's mask were the first artifacts sent to the Baseball Hall of Fame when the building opened in 1938.

THROW IT BACK!

If it ain't ours, you can have it back.

So say the Wrigley faithful who **defiantly throw all opposing teams' home run balls back onto the field.** They even hurl back the balls that make it out of the park onto Waveland or Sheffield avenues. Spectators wait patiently inside, and when the ballhawks on the street send that ball sailing back into the Friendly Confines, the dismay about the home run turns to cheers of appreciation for the Cubs fan outside.

This particular baseball tradition started at Wrigley Field—many say they believe it began in the 1980s—and has since been imitated at ballparks throughout the majors. But it's probably safe to say the passion of a Cubs fan sending a ball back to where it came from is unparalleled.

> The tradition of throwing back opposing hitters' home run balls almost certainly began in the 1980s; however, it was depicted in the 1977 play *Bleacher Bums*. And on one lonesome occasion, a 1969 Hank Aaron homer was thrown back onto the field.

TODAY, MANY OF THE BALLS TOSSED BACK ARE PROBABLY NOT THE ACTUAL HOME RUN BALL ITSELF BUT RATHER A NEW ONE, store-bought just in case the opportunity presents itself (after all, who doesn't want to bring home a souvenir?), but it's the action itself that really matters. Like we said, if it ain't ours, you can have it back.

BEST CUBS TRADES

- In 1982, the Cubs traded shortstop Ivan DeJesus to the Phillies for shortstop Larry Bowa and an unknown infielder named **Ryne Sandberg.**

- In 1992, the Cubs traded outfielder George Bell to the Chicago White Sox for relief pitcher Ken Patterson and some guy named **Sammy Sosa.**

- In November 1928, the Cubs traded Bruce Cunningham, Socks Seibold, Percy Jones, Lou Legett, Freddie Maguire, and $200,000 to the Braves for Rogers Hornsby, who hit .380 and helped the team win the pennant.

WORST CUBS TRADES

- In 1964, the Cubs traded future base-stealing champion and Hall of Fame outfielder **Lou Brock,** along with Jack Spring and Paul Toth, to the St. Louis Cardinals for Bobby Shantz, Doug Clemens, and 20-game winner Ernie Broglio, who promptly developed a sore arm.

- After the 1988 season, the Cubs traded **Rafael Palmeiro** (who hit more than 500 career home runs), **Jamie Moyer** (who was still pitching in the majors 20 years later), and Drew Hall to the Texas Rangers for Mitch "Wild Thing" Williams, Paul Kilgus, Steve Wilson, Curtis Wilkerson, Luis Benitez, and Pablo Delgado.

RANDY HUNDLEY'S FANTASY BASEBALL CAMP

According to former Cubs great Randy Hundley, this is the place where baseball fantasies come true. Ordinary, **everyday fans** (is there such a thing as an ordinary Cubs fan?) **suit up and take the field with a star-studded lineup of Cubs greats.** The roster typically includes former Hundley teammates, such as Ernie Banks, Ron Santo, Don Kessinger, Glenn Beckert, Billy Williams, and Fergie Jenkins—as well as stars from other squads throughout the years—Ryne Sandberg, Lee Smith, Rick Sutcliffe, and Jose Cardenal.

After an All-Star career in the majors followed by a stint as a minor-league manager, Hundley began holding baseball clinics for kids. Watching the fun and excitement that took place there, Hundley imagined a way to share that excitement with grown-up fans of the game. From this, the idea for the adult fantasy camp was born. Many copycat camps have sprung up since then, but none have matched the sensation of the original.

Since the early 1980s, Hundley's eight-day camp has been held each January in Mesa, Arizona, the Cubs spring training home. Participants must be at least 30 years old, but their level of skill, fitness, and experience are completely irrelevant—**all that's required of each camper is a love of the game.** Each year, about 115 to 125 fans sign on for a dream week of hanging out with their idols, soaking up baseball knowledge and experience.

Once at camp, participants don their own personalized Cubs uniforms and take the field alongside Hundley and crew for instruction and games. Living out the fantasy of every little kid, campers also receive a team photo, their own baseball card, a $1 million "contract" with the Cubs, an autographed ball, and a personalized Louisville Slugger bat. With plenty of action on the field, lots of chatter on the sidelines, and mingling during downtime, it's every Cubs fan's dream come true—their very own field of dreams.

THE 2003 CHICAGO CUBS
DESTINY OR DUSTINY?

What curse? That was the attitude of Cubs fans as the 2003 season wound down. They were wearing "In Dusty, We Trusty" T-shirts. In his first year at the helm of the Cubs, manager Dusty Baker seemed on the brink of doing something nobody had done for 95 years—bring the Cubs a World Series title.

With enthusiasm and excitement permeating the North Side, the Cubs played well during the 2003 regular season. Young starting pitchers **Kerry Wood and Mark Prior** seemed like the perfect one-two punch to lead the Cubs to that elusive world championship.

Any trip to the postseason is notable for the Cubs, but this was one season when fans thought big. It was not just about making the playoffs, it was about making *noise* in the playoffs. When the Cubs faced the Atlanta Braves in the National League Division Series, Wood won two games, Prior won one, and the Cubs survived three games to two. Heck, they even beat old friend Greg Maddux to nab the club's first postseason series triumph since the 1908 World Series.

The Cubs were playing terrific all-around baseball. In the next round, they faced the Florida Marlins, who, although they were not regarded as an intimidating foe, won the first game in the National League Championship Series. Stung, the Cubs roared back, won three straight, and were just one victory away from the World Series.

They dropped another game in Florida, but then the NLCS shifted to Wrigley Field. The Cubs could clinch on their home turf. Forget the goat!

The Cubs led Florida 3–0 in Game 6. Wrigley was rocking, the suspense was building, and Prior was cruising on the mound...until it all fell apart in a heartbeat after the infamous pop foul ball that Moises Alou couldn't quite grab, but fan Steve Bartman did. Alex Gonzalez made an error at short. Prior's pitches lost steam. The Marlins went on an eight-run tear, and suddenly the series was all tied up at three games apiece.

With Wood starting Game 7 at Wrigley, circumstances favored the Cubs, but a sense of foreboding took hold. Sure enough, the Cubs lost the decisive game and the Marlins went on to defeat the New York Yankees and capture the World Series title.

It was a crushing series of defeats, one that took the air of confidence out of the franchise and set in motion other bad karma. Wood and Prior suffered injuries. Baker seemed to lose his team. Sammy Sosa became more irritant than asset.

Faltering in 2003 haunted the Cubs and was not easily forgotten, but the Cubs would rebuild and find themselves back in the postseason just four years later.

"What was it, four or five years ago? You have to let it go. The best team won. The Marlins were the best team.... We didn't play good enough to win."

—Cubs third baseman Aramis Ramirez in 2008, when asked about 2003, *Chicago Tribune*

VINCE AND LOU—HOLY MACKEREL!

The late Vince Lloyd was affiliated with sports broadcasting on WGN radio from 1949 to 1987. He was most famous for sharing the microphone at Cubs games with Lou Boudreau, the Hall of Fame shortstop and former manager.

Lloyd spent more than 30 seasons handling Cubs radio broadcasts, doing color or play-by-play beginning in the early 1950s. He first shared the booth with Jack Brickhouse before pairing up with Boudreau. Vince and Lou worked together on Cubs games for 23 seasons. Lloyd had an energetic style, and when he saw something on the diamond that impressed him, he yelled, "Holy Mackerel!" When he did play-by-play, fans got their money's worth of description.

Born in the Chicago area, Boudreau was a prominent athlete in high school and at the University of Illinois before starring as a major-league shortstop from 1938 to 1952, primarily with the Cleveland Indians. He won the 1948 AL MVP Award while with the Indians and was an eight-time American League All-Star.

Boudreau thought he was done putting on flannels when he moved to the Cubs radio booth in 1960, but midway through that season, owner P. K. Wrigley insisted that Boudreau and Cubs manager Charlie Grimm switch places. The experiment only lasted until the end of the year, and Boudreau returned to the booth.

Vince and Lou were upbeat companions, and, in the 1970s, when a fan sent them a cowbell, it became a staple of their broadcasts. When a Cubs player hit a home run, they would clang the bell and declare, "That was a bell ringer!"

More appreciated as a color analyst than a play-by-play man, Boudreau sometimes goofed up names. He called Doug Rader "Radar" and more than once referred to Milt Pappas as "Pappish." Boudreau retired from broadcasting in 1988 when WGN did not renew his contract.

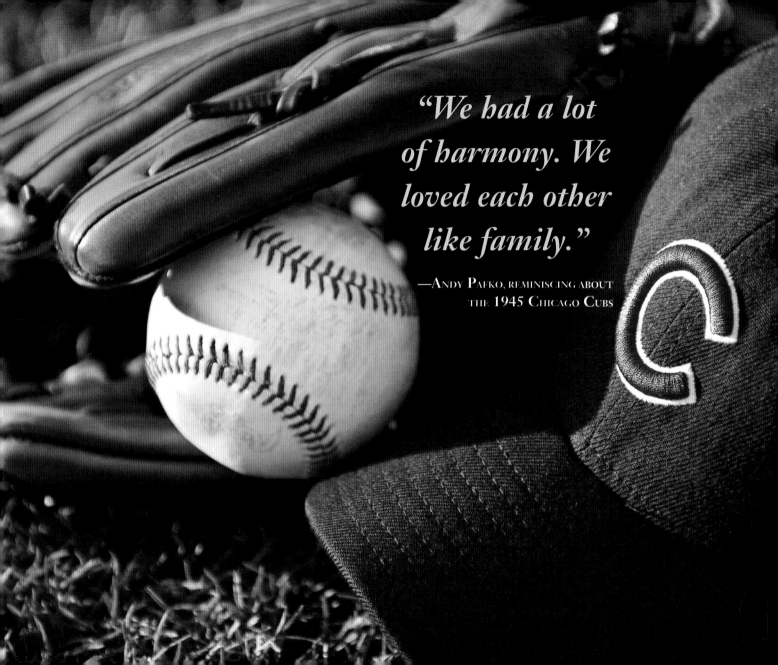

"We had a lot of harmony. We loved each other like family."

—ANDY PAFKO, REMINISCING ABOUT THE 1945 CHICAGO CUBS

JUMBOTRONS AND EXPLODING SCOREBOARDS?
NOT AT WRIGLEY FIELD

Other ballparks around the league (okay, *all* other ballparks around the league) have huge, modern electronic scoreboards with all the latest bells and whistles. Some actually *do* whistle—if that's what you call the noise that fireworks make while shooting out of the board. They all have fancy screens, offering fans a steady diet of clever graphics, player stats, and instant replays.

And certainly these features have their merits, but at Wrigley Field, fans are treated to something different. Standing statuesque and proud at an impressive 75 feet wide and 27 feet tall, the park's famous **hand-operated scoreboard**—the last in existence in major-league parks—embodies all the vintage charm and character of the storied park.

No batted ball has ever struck the scoreboard (although Hall of Famer Roberto Clemente and Cubs slugger Bill Nicholson both came close), but golf champion Sam Snead once teed up a golf ball at home plate and sent it sailing into the board.

CONSTRUCTION OF THIS WRIGLEY LANDMARK TOOK PLACE DURING THE MAMMOTH RENOVATION OF 1937–38, in which the 1914 ballpark got a makeover that included the addition of the scoreboard, the bleachers, and the ivy on the outfield wall. The ten-foot-diameter clock was added in 1941.

Located behind the bleachers, straightaway from home plate, the famed scoreboard displays all the day's (or night's) pertinent information without any gimmicks or gadgets. National League inning-by-inning game action is listed on the left, American League on the right. The Cubs' own game occupies a cozy corner on the bottom left of the board.

Prominent in the center of the board are niches that display the batter's number, balls, strikes, outs, hits, and errors. The scoreboard operators perch themselves inside the board to follow the game with a watchful eye from what are certainly some of the best seats in the house. Every time a ball or strike is called, the operator touches the electronic button to post it on the board. **Numbered tiles are changed manually as runs are scored each inning.**

Every day, the flags of all the National League teams are hoisted from the center-field pole to reflect the standings. And speaking of flags, no fan can miss the white "W" flag that flies from the scoreboard to let those passing by on the street or from the El train know when the Cubbies have come out on top.

And so this historic scoreboard holds court over Wrigley Field, despite the addition of the bold and flashy TV screens to all the other parks. One concession to the times has been the small electronic board that runs beneath the Wrigley

Field scoreboard displaying the batter's name along with his stats (RBI, hits, and batting average). It's a small compromise that brings more information to the crowd while keeping the treasured old scoreboard in its rightful place of honor and prominence.

RON SANTO'S SECRET

Ron Santo manned third base with distinction for the Cubs for 14 seasons from 1960 to 1973. Even more impressive was that Santo competed while suffering from Type 1 diabetes. He required insulin shots for the chronic disease but never complained and was determined to keep his illness secret.

Diagnosed as an 18-year-old and told by a doctor he wouldn't live past 25, **Santo never wanted diabetes to become an issue in his career,** and he never wanted to be put in a situation where he might be forced to retire because of the illness.

Santo even kept the fact that he had the debilitating illness hidden from his roommate, second baseman Glenn Beckert—until the day Beckert saw Santo injecting an insulin shot. The incident occurred during one of Santo's hot streaks, and Beckert, thinking his friend was using some type of artificial substance to enhance his abilities, jokingly asked for some of the same.

"What are those medications you're taking?" Beckert said, confronting Santo. "I need some of that."

Santo then told Beckert about his diabetes. However, it was not until August 28, 1971—Ron Santo Day at Wrigley Field—that Santo went public about his challenges from diabetes.

Santo recounts a story from a 1968 game against the Dodgers during which he experienced dizziness in the on-deck circle and saw the scoreboard in triplicate. Blurred vision made stepping into the batter's box against fire-balling pitcher Bill Singer a potentially dangerous situation for Santo. But amazingly, he overcame that obstacle and hit a grand slam to win the game 4–1.

"All I had to do was circle the bases," Santo said, "and I wasn't sure where they were."

Since his playing days, Santo has become more forthcoming about his disease and the terrible toll it has taken on his body (he's had parts of

Ron Santo signs an autograph at his 2006 Walk to Cure Diabetes.

both legs amputated), and he has worked tirelessly in the Chicago community to raise money for diabetes research. Every year, the former Cub helps to organize an event called the **Ron Santo Walk to Cure Diabetes,** with proceeds going to the Juvenile Diabetes Research Foundation, which works to find a cure for the disease. The 30th annual walk was held October 5, 2008, and since its inception, the walk has contributed more than $50 million to the charity.

Santo is now an inspiration to those with diabetes and to athletes who have overcome obstacles. As a touching tribute to the legendary player, Ron's son Jeff filmed a documentary about his father's life called *This Old Cub*, which was released in 2004.

In recent voting by the Veterans Committee, Santo has come close to election to the Baseball Hall of Fame, but to no avail. So, on September 28, 2003, when the Cubs retired Santo's No. 10 jersey, he exuberantly declared to a packed house at Wrigley Field, "This is my Hall of Fame!"

"JO-DY! JO-DY!" JODY DAVIS

Something about young catcher Jody Davis caught the eye of Harry Caray, and in 1983, Davis's second full season with the club, the Cubs announcer began to root him on intently. What did Harry see in Davis that he liked so much? It couldn't have been his defense, which was shaky early on in his career. He was definitely tearing it up at the plate, though, hitting .271 with 24 home runs. But Caray had noticed something more. This kid was Caray's kind of player—someone who took his place on the field every day and maintained a great attitude, working hard and giving his teammates a boost. And the fans loved him, too, chanting "Jo-dy! Jo-dy! Jo-dy!" whenever he stepped up to the plate.

Davis, who joined the team in 1981, worked hard behind the plate for the Cubs before being traded to the Atlanta Braves midway through the '88 season. He was **a key figure on the 1984 squad, helping end the team's 39-year playoff drought.** That was also the year he earned the first of his two All-Star selections. The defensively challenged catcher worked hard to improve his game, so much so that he garnered **a Gold Glove Award in '86**—something nobody would have ever thought possible for a guy who had piled up errors and passed balls throughout his career. But that was the kind of player Davis was—a hard worker who did what it took to get the job done. That was why Harry, the fans, and the Cubs organization loved him. And those leadership qualities that were so evident during his playing days led the Cubs to hire him back as a minor-league manager in the mid-2000s—to teach their young players to play hard and get the job done.

MAJOR LEAGUE TOTALS			
G	HR	RBI	BA
1,082	127	490	.245

CUBS QUIZ

1. Since the 2007 season, what song has been played at Wrigley Field after each home victory?

. . . .

2. Which **prominent hitter from the powerhouse 1927 New York Yankees** was briefly part of the Cubs' roster near the end of his career? (Hint: He's pictured on the left.)

. . . .

3. What is the name of the organ player at Wrigley Field?

. . . .

4. What killed Cubs broadcaster Jack Quinlan?

5. What number did Hall of Famer **Billy Williams** wear for his first two seasons in 1959 and 1960?

6. What was colorful first baseman Joe Pepitone's most dramatic move during the 1972 season?

1. "Go Cubs Go" by Steve Goodman; 2. Tony Lazzeri played 54 games with the Cubs in 1938; 3. Gary Pressy; 4. While in Arizona for spring training in 1965, Quinlan was returning to the team hotel after playing golf, when he lost control of his car and crashed into a tractor trailer; 5. Williams, whose future No. 26 was retired by the Cubs, originally wore No. 4; 6. Pepitone retired in the middle of the season to run his bar, Joe Pepitone's Thing, but came out of retirement after only 60 days. He never hit well for the Cubs again.

CHAPTER SIX

"YOU'RE MY CUBS"

"It's a beautiful day for a ball game;

Out in the bright sunshine.

I'm on my way out to Wrigley Field,

To be with that team of mine.

I hear the call of the ivy on the wall,

God's own green grass, let's play ball!"

— MUSIC AND LYRICS BY ALAN BARCUS

Geovany Soto

"*I stepped on the grass at Wrigley Field, and I felt like I was walking on air....I knew...I was in the right place.*"

—CUBS THIRD BASEMAN RON SANTO ON HIS LOVE OF WRIGLEY FIELD

"Ryne Sandberg is the best baseball player I've ever seen.... He's Baby Ruth."

—CARDINALS MANAGER WHITEY HERZOG AFTER SANDBERG'S DISPLAY ON JUNE 23, 1984

SWEET-SWINGIN' BILLY WILLIAMS

Billy Williams is a quiet guy from Whistler, Alabama, a small town on the outskirts of the baseball hotbed of Mobile. (Among the other superstars who came out of Mobile were pitcher Satchel Paige and Hank Aaron.) Billy grew up fishing with his brothers and playing baseball on the sandlots. Buck O'Neil, the one-time star player and manager of the Kansas City Monarchs of the Negro Leagues, spotted Williams for the Cubs. The team signed Williams in 1956. Throughout his career with the Cubs, the man with the "sweet swing" teamed with fellow Hall of Famer Ernie Banks in the greatest one-two offensive punch in team history.

Williams first arrived in the Cubs' lineup for a short stint in 1959 and another the next year. By 1961, he was not only a regular on the squad, he was also the National League's Rookie of the Year. Reliable, dependable, and exceptionally talented, Williams rarely missed a game. Although

he could—and did—deliver the spectacular, he was known for his remarkable consistency, hitting 20 or more home runs for 13 straight seasons and playing in 157 or more games each year from 1962 through 1971. At one point, the sweet-swinging lefty played in 1,117 consecutive games—a National League record (since topped by Steve Garvey).

Throughout the 1960s and '70s, one thing Cubs fans could count on was Billy Williams. The six-time All-Star actually seemed to get

"I always felt that my swing came naturally. I was blessed in that respect."

—Billy Williams, from *My Sweet-Swinging Lifetime with the Cubs* by Billy Williams and Fred Mitchell

MAJOR LEAGUE TOTALS			
G	**HR**	**RBI**	**BA**
2,488	426	1,475	.290

better with age, topping the NL with 137 runs scored in 1970—then the highest total in the league since 1947. He nearly won the Triple Crown in '72, with 37 homers, 122 RBI, and a .333 batting average. Although he lost the MVP title to Johnny Bench, he was awarded the Silver Bat Award by NL President Charles Feeney.

On June 29, 1969, more than 40,000 fans honored him at a Wrigley Field doubleheader dubbed "Billy Williams Day," cheering him on as he surpassed Stan Musial on the all-time list of consecutive games played with 896. He also cracked five hits in the twin bill—not a bad day.

"That day will stick out in my memory for many, many years," Williams later recalled.

Although he never reached the postseason in his career with the Cubs, he did finally make it with the A's in 1975. He continues to serve the Cubs as a special assistant to the president, and his retired No. 26, which flies from a flag on the right-field foul pole, is a constant reminder of his quiet excellence.

WRIGLEYVILLE'S NEIGHBORHOOD HAUNTS

- **Bernie's Tap & Grill**
  - Casey Moran's
  - The Cubby Bear
  - Sports Corner
  - Vines on Clark
  - Yak-Zies

- **Harry Caray's Tavern**
  - John Barleycorn

- **Murphy's Bleachers**
  - Sluggers
  - The Dugout Bar and Grill
  - Goose Island Wrigleyville

MERKLE'S BONER

On September 23, 1908, the Cubs trailed the New York Giants in the standings by a half game when the two teams squared off at the Polo Grounds. With the score tied at 1–1 and two outs in the bottom of the ninth, Moose McCormick of the Giants was on third, and young rookie Fred Merkle was on first. When New York's Al Bridwell singled, the crowd exploded as McCormick trotted home to score what appeared to be the winning run. Fans poured onto the field in jubilation, and Merkle headed for the clubhouse. Realizing that Merkle hadn't stepped on second, Johnny Evers called frantically for the ball and stepped on the bag for the force-out—according to major-league rules, the run shouldn't count.

When Giants fans began to realize what had happened, mayhem broke out on the field. Umpire Hank O'Day had to be rescued from the melee and escorted out of the park by the police. The next day, O'Day followed up with a written report to the National League office, in which he called Merkle out on a force play and declared the game a 1–1 tie. The Giants furiously filed a protest, but National League officials backed O'Day's decision.

"The good Lord puts you on earth to become a professional baseball player, and he says it's going to be up to you to play hard and be successful."

—1940s Cubs star Phil Cavarretta, from *Banks to Sandberg to Grace* by Carrie Muskat

SLAMMIN' SAMMY GETS BEANED

This was no way to treat your hometown hero. Pirates pitcher Salomon Torres grew up in San Pedro de Macoris, the same Dominican Republic town that produced Cubs slugger Sammy Sosa. Before an April 20, 2003, game in Pittsburgh, Torres and Sosa exchanged warm greetings.

"He's like an idol to me," Torres said.

Sosa had already homered off Josh Fogg in the first inning, and Torres relieved an injured Fogg in the second. Pitching to his idol in the fourth, Torres unleashed a fastball that struck Sosa on the left earflap of his helmet. The helmet made a loud crack and shattered, as Sosa went to the ground with cuts on his ear and temple.

"That was one of the worst helmet cracks I've seen or heard," said Cubs manager Dusty Baker, a baseball veteran. "I'm surprised he was conscious."

Sosa walked off the field slowly and was taken to Allegheny Hospital for X-rays that showed no fractures. He returned to the lineup two days later against San Diego.

Torres said he did not hit Sosa intentionally. Sosa felt the same way. "The helmet saved me," he said.

CUBS ROTATION TAKES
A WINNING TURN IN 2008

Not long ago, it was Kerry Wood and Mark Prior around whom the Cubs planned to build their rotation of the future. But in 2008, it was a starting staff without either of those power-pitching names that took the majors by storm.

Carlos Zambrano, Ryan Dempster, Ted Lilly, and Jason Marquis formed the yearlong nucleus, and the midseason addition of Rich Harden in a trade with the A's struck further fear into opposing hitters. Together, the group led Chicago to its best season in decades.

Here's a brief look at the men who formed one of the best starting rotations in the majors.

Carlos Zambrano, RHP. "Big Z" won seven straight decisions in April, May, and June to get the Cubs started toward a divisional lead. With a 14–6 record in 2008, he won 13 or more games for the sixth straight season, all in a Cubs uniform, and continued to help his own cause as one of the best-hitting pitchers in recent years, smacking four home runs in 2008, allowing him to overtake Fergie Jenkins as the most prolific home run hitting pitcher in Cubs history.

Rich Harden, RHP. A day after the rival Brewers traded for pitching ace CC Sabathia, the Cubs answered by landing Harden in a six-player deal. The hard-throwing righty had been 5–1 with a 2.34 ERA for

the A's, and he continued to blow hitters away in his National League debut. Harden compiled a 5–1 record with a 1.77 ERA for the Cubs, including five games with ten or more strikeouts.

Ted Lilly, LHP. Every top rotation needs a strong southpaw, and Lilly fits the bill. Although he started off 1–4, he finished strong with a 17–9 record overall—his sixth consecutive year with 10 or more wins. Lilly put together one of the most dominant stretches of his career in midseason, winning eight of nine decisions during May and June.

Ryan Dempster, RHP. Few experiments have gone better than Dempster's conversion from closer to starter. He reached a career high 17 wins and was virtually unbeatable at home, posting a 14–3 record at Wrigley Field.

Jason Marquis, RHP. One of the best fifth starters in baseball, Marquis could be a No. 1 starter for other clubs. Once a 15-game winner and Silver Slugger Award recipient with the Cardinals, he went 11–9 in 2008, won five straight decisions in May and June, and held down his number of home runs allowed to keep giving the Cubs a chance to win ball games.

1908 WORLD SERIES CHAMPIONS

As the 1908 Cubs were gritting out a tough pennant race—perhaps the most competitive of all time—scrapping their way to a second consecutive world championship, no one imagined that 1908 would become such a watershed year for the team.

> Ironically, 90 years after the Cubs and Giants squared off in a tie-breaking game to decide who would go to the 1908 World Series, the two teams met again in a one-game showdown to determine entry into the 1998 postseason. The Cubs also won that game 5–3.

The defending world champs came back for the '08 season poised for another great showing. They won the opener 6–5 over Cincinnati to set the tone and, in the season's early weeks, enjoyed fine outings from key pitchers Orval Overall (a two-hitter over the Cardinals) and Mordecai "Three Finger" Brown (a one-hitter to beat the Dodgers).

The team was loaded with talent, most notably the double-play combo of Tinker to Evers to Chance, catcher Johnny Kling, and hard-hitting outfielder Frank Shulte. And the pitching squad of Brown (29 wins), Overall (15 wins), and Ed Reulbach (24 wins) was unmatched.

Sure, the Cubs had the goods to repeat, but that did not mean the '08 season was a cakewalk. The '06 and '07 squads had bolted out of the gates to huge leads, but this campaign proved to be a much tougher race. The Cubs were neck and neck with the New York Giants and Pittsburgh Pirates all season long, and tensions were running high. In June, a brawl broke out between outfielder Jimmy Sheckard and infielder Heinie Zimmerman that roiled through the clubhouse.

As tumultuous as clubhouse relations were, on-field doings were just as confusing. Throughout August and September, the three teams jockeyed for position, with the Cubs slipping as far as four games out. On September 23, only a half game separated the Cubs from the first-place Giants when they met at the Polo Grounds. The infamous hard-fought game ended in a tie as a result of a play known as "Merkle's Boner."

The Cubs, Giants, and Pirates had all played above-.700 ball through September and October, but the Pirates finished a half game out. The Cubs and Giants ended the season in a deadlock, so a tie-breaking game determined the outcome of the September 23 contest. Merkle's Boner had made all the difference. The Cubs went on to win the tie-breaker 4–2 to claim the pennant.

In comparison with the excitement and drama of the pennant run, the 1908 World Series was easy. The Cubs defeated the Detroit Tigers four games to one. Tinker recorded the first home run ever by a Cub in the World Series, and Brown and Overall hurled shutouts in Games 4 and 5. The last game, which was played in Detroit, attracted only 6,210 fans—an all-time low for a World Series game. The one hour, twenty-five-minute contest was also the shortest in Series history.

If the Cubs had known that this would be their last World Series victory for at least 100 years, they might have dragged the game out a little longer.

Detroit's Ty Cobb hits against the Cubs in the 1908 World Series.

THE SANDBERG GAME

June 23, 1984. Ask any die-hard Cubs fan the significance of that date and a nostalgic smile will sweep across his or her face. Simply known as "The Sandberg Game," the legendary game lives on in team lore as **one of the greatest displays of clutch hitting in team history.** It was also a most explosive day at the plate for young second baseman Ryne Sandberg. And it didn't hurt that the performance came against the rival St. Louis Cardinals.

In June of '84, Sandberg was in his third full season with the Cubs and on his way to his first All-Star Game. Although the team was five games over .500, this showdown with the Redbirds was a pivotal moment. The Cubs had been slumping, losing six of their previous eight games, and it seemed the season could tilt either way. Sandberg made sure the arrow pointed up.

Ryno didn't set any batting records that day, but the event is one of the most memorable games in Cubs history, not only for Sandberg's performance, but also for the point in the game when he rose to the occasion. The second base-man **blasted two home runs and three singles while driving in seven runs in an 11-inning, 12–11 Cubs victory.** The nationally televised game showcased Sandberg at his best and the Cubs at their most dramatic.

After trailing 7–1 in what was shaping up to be a depressing wipeout, the Cubs had rallied to within one run going into the bottom of the ninth. The Cardinals brought in their closer, future Hall of Famer Bruce Sutter, who had a 1.16 ERA at the time.

Sandberg smacked his first homer off Sutter in the bottom of the ninth to tie the game 9–9, sending it into extra innings. When the Cardinals moved ahead 11–9 in the tenth, Sandberg marched to the plate in the bottom of the frame and again slammed a home run—this time a two-run job—to tie the score again. The Cubs won in the next inning when Leon Durham walked, stole second, went to third on an error, and then was driven home by a single from Dave Owen. The Cubs played terrific baseball from then on, going 59–34 during the remainder of the season to qualify for their first postseason in 39 years.

A nine-time Gold Glove winner, ten-time All-Star, and Class of 2005 Hall of Fame inductee, Sandberg has a résumé of highlights a mile long, but invariably, when

he bumps into fans and baseball people (except for Bruce Sutter, of course), they always want to talk about that game. When asked how often it has come up in conversation, Sandberg laughed and said, "About a million times."

The fact that the game was on NBC certainly enhanced the viewing audience, but Sandberg has said many times that he can't get over how that day has resonated with Cubs fans. He said the only thing he remembers differently from the average fan is that he doesn't call it "The Sandberg Game." To him it was "The Bruce Sutter Game."

KOSUKE FUKUDOME

After the 2007 season, the Cubs went shopping in Japan for a new right fielder and signed established star Kosuke Fukudome to a four-year deal. Fukudome's first spring training with the club was a quiet one—except for the hordes of media following his every move.

But once the Cubs began the season, Fukudome exploded into the fans' consciousness, producing excitement with his bat and on the field from the start. On Opening Day, he hit a double in his first at bat then cracked a three-run homer against the Milwaukee Brewers in the bottom of the ninth to send the game into extra innings. The Cubs lost 4–3 in ten innings, but the one-time star for Chunichi of the Japanese Central League went 3-for-3 in his debut, making him an overnight sensation. His strong work ethic, discipline at the plate, and excellence on the field earned him a starting spot in the All-Star Game during what Major League Baseball considered his rookie season.

Fans embraced Fukudome not only with cheers but also with signs penned in Japanese and English. However, in some cases, just as actor Bill Murray found in the movie *Lost in Translation*, there was a bit of a communication gap. The English side of one sign read, "It's gonna happen." But on the flip side, in Japanese, the sign read, "It's an accident."

On the contrary, everything Fukudome did on the diamond seemed to be quite purposeful, even if his second-half numbers didn't live up to the club's (or the fans') expectations.

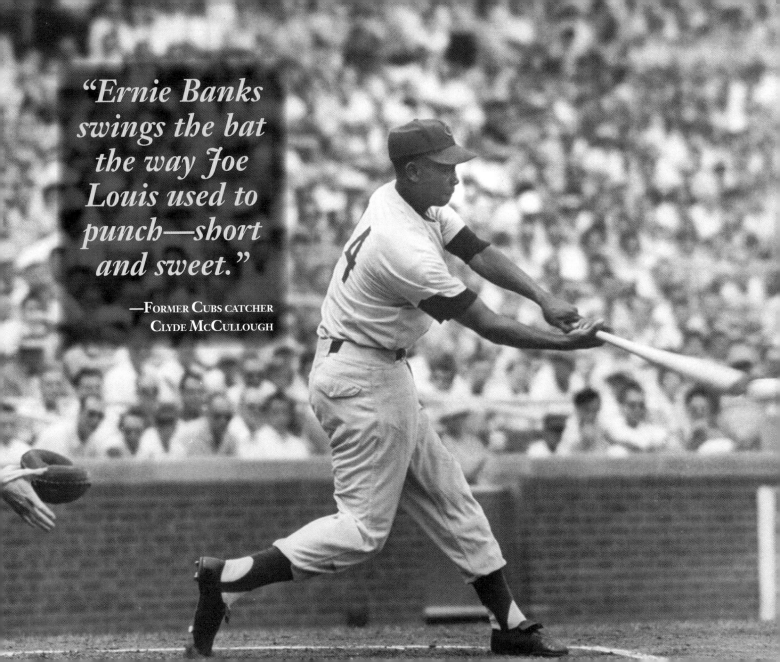

"*Ernie Banks swings the bat the way Joe Louis used to punch—short and sweet.*"

—Former Cubs catcher Clyde McCullough

MAJOR LEAGUE TOTALS					
G	W	L	SO	SV	ERA
1,022	71	92	1,251	478	3.03

"BIG LEE" SMITH

For most of Lee Smith's 18-season career as a closer, beginning when he came up with the Cubs in 1980, he was **the epitome of unhittable.** He stood 6′6″ and weighed 225 pounds, and when his fastball was at its peak, his 95-mile-per-hour bullets could barely be seen. The flamethrower overpowered hitters in his stints out of the bullpen and four times led the league in saves—three times in the National League and once in the American.

Smith spent eight seasons with the Cubs before being shipped to the Red Sox in 1988. He was a seven-time All-Star during his career (twice while with the Cubs), and when he retired after the 1997 campaign, he owned the all-time saves record of 478, a mark he kept until Trevor Hoffman surpassed it in 2006. During his heyday, **Smith was the master of intimidating hitters,** starting with his slow stroll from the bullpen to the mound and ending with his specialty—a blazing fastball that led to more than 1,200 late-inning strikeouts.

After he retired, Smith worked as a roving pitching instructor for the San Francisco Giants and served as a pitching coach for the South African national team at the 2006 World Baseball Classic. Despite being the record-holder for saves for years, upon eligibility for the Baseball Hall of Fame, Smith garnered only minimal support for enshrinement, a baffling development and one that disturbed him.

CUBS SPRING TRAINING LOCATIONS THROUGH THE YEARS

- 1900—Selma, Alabama

- 1901–02—Champaign, Illinois

- 1903–04—Los Angeles, California

- 1905—Santa Monica, California

- 1906–08—West Baden, Indiana

- 1909—Shreveport, Louisiana

- 1910–11—West Baden, Indiana

- 1912—New Orleans, Louisiana

- 1913–16—Tampa, Florida

- 1917–20—Pasadena, California

- 1921–41—Catalina Island, California

- 1942–45—French Lick, Indiana

- 1946–51—Catalina Island, California

- 1952–65—Mesa, Arizona

- 1966—Long Beach, California

- 1967–78—Scottsdale, Arizona

- 1979–Present—Mesa, Arizona

"LITTLE LARRY" CORCORAN

Time has dimmed his name in Cubs lore, but Larry Corcoran was a dominant pitcher for the team between 1880 and 1885. Although the rules were not precisely the same in his day as they are today, Corcoran **threw the first three no-hitters in Cubs history,** one each in 1880, 1882, and 1884. The diminutive right-handed hurler—he was 5′3″ and weighed around 125 pounds—won 27 or more games five times for the Cubs but burned out quickly from overuse. As a 20-year-old rookie in 1880, Corcoran threw a remarkable 536⅓ innings. However, not surprisingly, he soon developed arm injuries and finished his time in the majors in 1887 with India-napolis. Despite a short career, Corcoran is **credited with being one of the first pitchers to throw a curveball and to develop signs with his catcher** to signal what pitches to throw.

MAJOR LEAGUE TOTALS				
G	W	L	SO	ERA
277	177	89	1,103	2.36

CARLOS Z-RIFFIC IN HISTORIC NO-NO

The setting was unusual. The timing was unpredictable. And Carlos Zambrano was unhittable.

Zambrano became the first Cubs pitcher since Milt Pappas in 1972 to throw a no-hitter when he stifled the Houston Astros 5–0 before 23,441 fans on September 14, 2008, at Miller Park in Milwaukee.

The game—technically a home contest for the Astros despite a loudly pro-Cubs crowd—was moved to Milwaukee when Hurricane Ike blew through the Houston area. Zambrano then blew away the Astros, becoming the first man in major-league history to throw a no-hitter in a park that was home to neither team.

Few saw it coming. While "Big Z" was a dominant force for much of the season, he had missed his previous start with tendinitis in his right shoulder. The game against Houston was his first in 12 days.

"I guess I'm back," he deadpanned after allowing only two balls to leave the infield all night. He did not need spectacular plays or a stroke of good fortune. His fastball (which reached 98 miles per hour), split-finger pitch, and slider were more than enough. Ten Astros went down on strikes and one walked on Zambrano's 110-pitch night.

"He had everything going," Cubs manager Lou Piniella said. "From the first few pitches of the ball game, you could tell his arm was live."

The following day, the Cubs made more history when Ted Lilly held Houston hitless into the seventh inning. Mark Loretta singled to break up the no-hit bid—the only hit Cubs pitchers yielded all day. It was the first time in major-league history a team followed a no-hitter with a one-hitter.

ZAMBRANO VS. HOUSTON					
IP	H	R	ER	BB	SO
9	0	0	0	1	10

"MAD DOG": BILL MADLOCK

When Bill Madlock came to the Cubs before the 1974 season, in the deal that sent Fergie Jenkins to Texas, the Cubs thought they'd found a long-term replacement for Ron Santo at third base.

In 1975, during his second year with the North Siders, Madlock hit a National League-leading .354 to nail down his first batting title.

But near the end of the next season, on a road trip to New York, Madlock was beaten up in his hotel room and robbed of $50. He was sidelined with headaches for several games before returning to the lineup to go 4-for-4 on the season's final day and win the batting title again with a .339 average.

However, angered by his salary demands, the Cubs foolishly dumped Madlock in an off-season trade with San Francisco that brought Bobby Murcer and Steve Ontiveros to the team before the 1977 campaign. The Cubs, who were unable to replace Madlock's bat, were only able to watch in dismay as he won a World Championship with the Pittsburgh Pirates in 1979 as well as two more batting crowns to cap off a 15-year career that produced a .305 lifetime batting average.

"THUNDER PUP"
SHAWON DUNSTON

A COLORFUL PLAYER WHO PLAYED A FLASHY SHORTSTOP AND TALKED A GOOD GAME, Shawon Dunston broke into the majors with the Cubs in 1985 and played 18 major-league seasons with an enduring passion for the sport.

The No. 1 overall pick in the 1982 draft, Dunston was known for his lightning fast (but often wild) arm, blazing speed (he had eight seasons of double-digit steals for the Cubs), and propensity to swing at anything (he racked up 1,000 strikeouts in his career). Nicknamed "Thunder Pup," the two-time All-Star also created excitement with timely home runs and clutch RBI and was a fan favorite for a decade, until injuries contributed to his departure from Chicago in 1996. Having spent time on six different teams, Dunston still maintains that Chicago is easily the best place to play.

Who doesn't remember the "Shawon-O-Meter"—a popular sign flaunted in the bleachers that kept track of Shawon's rising and falling batting average?

BASEBALL'S HIGHEST SCORING GAME

On August 25, 1922, the highest scoring game in major-league history was contested in Cubs Park. **Chicago defeated the Philadelphia Phillies 26–23** that day, and despite the football-like score, the game did not involve any touchdowns or extra points.

Although there were **51 hits during the game, only three of them were home runs,** a reflection of the state of baseball as the dead-ball era was winding down, Babe Ruth was transforming hitting approaches, and the lively ball era was just getting started.

The Cubs took leads of 25–6 and 26–9 but had to withstand a 14-run Phillies rally spread over the eighth and ninth innings. During the slugfest, the Cubs also established a team record for runs scored in a single inning by putting 14 runs on the board in the fourth inning.

CUBS RECORDS

- Slugging percentage—.590—Hack Wilson

- Runs scored—1,719—Cap Anson

- Triples—142—Jimmy Ryan

- Walks—1,092—Stan Hack

- Stolen bases—400—Frank Chance

- Complete games (since 1900)—206—Mordecai "Three-Finger" Brown

- Innings pitched—3,137⅓—Charlie Root

- Most years pitching—16—Charlie Root

- Most games started pitching—347—Ferguson Jenkins

- Fielding percentage for catchers—.992—Randy Hundley

- Fielding chances (all positions)—18,235—Mark Grace

SMILING STAN HACK

Before there was Ernie Banks, there was "Smiling" Stan Hack, possessor of the sunniest disposition at Wrigley Field. Although it must have been frustrating to reach the World Series four times without ever bringing home a championship, Smiling Stan just kept smiling, and he gave Cubs fans something to grin about, too.

Hack broke in with the Cubs in 1932 and spent his entire big-league career—16 seasons—with the club. The stellar third baseman was a team leader and, for much of his career, a league leader. A five-time All-Star, Hack was a great contact hitter and leadoff man who walked twice as often as he struck out. He led the league in stolen bases and hits twice, hit over .300 six times, and led third basemen in fielding in 1942 and '45.

After his retirement in 1947, the immensely popular third baseman returned to manage the team from 1954 to 1956. His managerial skills proved less than stellar, and the Cubs never came close to a winning record under his leadership. Smiling Stan, who helped lead four teams to the pennant, never did bring a world championship flag home to Wrigley Field.

"Tall, slender, handsome, confident— Hack was the idol of every sandlot urchin playing third base in a pair of torn knickers."

—Author William Curran

SOME NOTABLE WORLD EVENTS SINCE THE CUBS' 1908 WORLD SERIES TITLE

- World War I—1914–18

- Communists take over Russia and create the Soviet Union—1917

- **The National Football League is organized—1920**

- Babe Ruth sets a single-season home-run record of 60—1927

- Alexander Fleming discovers penicillin—1928

- Franklin Delano Roosevelt elected president of the United States four times—1932, 1936, 1940, and 1944

- World War II—1939–45

- **The National Basketball Association is organized—1946**

- **Elvis Presley revolutionizes rock 'n' roll with his first No. 1 hit "Heartbreak Hotel"—1956**

- Don Larsen of the New York Yankees pitches a perfect game in the World Series—1956

- The Boston Celtics win 11 titles in 13 seasons—1957–69

- Roger Maris breaks Babe Ruth's single-season home-run record with 61—1961

- **The United States puts a man on the moon through space travel—1969**

- The Berlin Wall falls, representing the fall of Communism in Eastern Europe—1989

- Mark McGwire breaks Roger Maris's single-season home-run record of 61 by slugging 70—1998

- Barry Bonds breaks Mark McGwire's record with 73—2001

WRIGLEY'S HAUNTS
ALWAYS IN ATTENDANCE

Balls that disappear into the ivy, never to be seen again. Phone calls originating from a seemingly empty dugout. Voices, shadows, and lights in the night. All are part of the Wrigley Field mystique, and none has been adequately explained—unless you believe in ghosts.

Dan Gordon and Mickey Bradley wrote a book called *Haunted Baseball*, which explores ghost stories from diamonds across the land. When asked which stadium is the most haunted, Gordon replied, "Wrigley Field." **Charlie Grimm,** a former Cubs player who managed the team in the 1930s and '40s, is mentioned often as the culprit when the unexplained occurs. His ashes are reportedly buried in a box in the outfield, and his ghost is accused of having cast shadows, whispered names, and turned on stadium lights during the night.

Frequently, **stadium workers and even team members have reported hearing the bullpen phone ring.** That would not normally be cause for concern, except that the phone is a direct line from the Cubs dugout—the only place such a call could originate—and, you guessed it, the dugout always stood empty when these calls came through. Or did it?

"The story is that Charlie Grimm is calling the bullpen again," Marty Moore, a longtime Wrigley Field security guard, told Gordon and Bradley. "It's very eerie when you are here by yourself."

Sometimes, Wrigley Field is eerie even when packed with fans. Players who throw their arms up when a ball rolls into the ivy covering the outfield walls concede a ground rule double to the opposition. Some of those balls, however, are never found again.

Is that Grimm, too? Or is it Steve Goodman, a die-hard Cubs fan and songwriter who penned the Arlo Guthrie hit "City of New Orleans," as well as "Go Cubs Go" and "A Dying Cubs Fan's Last Request," a song about a Cubs fan planning a funeral at home plate in which his ashes are scattered? Goodman died at age 36, just four

days before the 1984 Cubs clinched their division, sending them to the postseason for the first time in 39 years. Or could the mischievous spirit be the ghost of longtime broadcaster Harry Caray, whose death in February 1998 preceded a rare successful season for the Cubs and had the team bring in paranormal researchers? Not surprisingly, those ghost hunters found significant "activity" in the bleachers.

Perhaps, someday, a voice on the bullpen phone will provide some answers.

CHEER, CHEER FOR "THE SHARK"
JEFF SAMARDZIJA

Chicago might be home to more Notre Dame football fans than any city in the United States, including South Bend, Indiana. And we know how Chicagoans, particularly those on the North Side, love their Cubs.

So it was a match made in heaven when former record-setting Notre Dame wide receiver Jeff Samardzija debuted as a Cubs pitcher during the 2008 season.

As a freshman, some of Samardzija's Fighting Irish baseball teammates affectionately nicknamed him "The Shark" because they thought he resembled the shark in Disney's *Finding Nemo*. Notre Dame opponents were not so happy to become his prey.

On the diamond, Samardzija went 21–6 over three seasons, posting 8–1 and 8–2 records in his final two years. As a football All-American and Brady Quinn's favorite target, he set season and career records at Notre Dame for receiving yards while catching touchdown passes in a school-record eight consecutive games.

Drafted by the Cubs in the fifth round in 2006, Samardzija pitched in the minors, played one final season of college football, and made his major-league debut on July 25, 2008—just 19 months after catching his final pass in a Notre Dame uniform.

Hitting the upper 90s on the radar gun, he struck out the first batter he faced, Florida's Alfredo Amezaga, bringing 41,570 Wrigley Field fans to their feet. Though he allowed a late home run in a Cubs loss that day, Samardzija brought the heat again in his next outing two days later to hold off the Marlins for his first major-league save.

Afterward, manager Lou Piniella joked that he might have finally found a connection for hard-to-get Notre Dame football tickets. "But I don't want to sit in the upper deck," he quipped.

Samardzija, after promising to bring his manager along on a sideline pass to a Notre Dame game, turned his attention back to his professional sport of choice.

"I couldn't ask for anything more," he said.

LET THERE BE LIGHT

8/8/88. It's a date all Cubs fans can reel off without a second thought. It's the date Wrigley Field and the Cubs were thrust into the spotlight—literally.

For nearly three-quarters of a century, Wrigley Field opened its gates for day games only. While night baseball came to the majors in 1931 (for an exhibition game in Houston) and was here to stay by 1935, when the Cincinnati Reds' Crosley Field was illuminated, Wrigley Field remained the only stadium where baseball was always played in the light of day.

The lights had almost been turned on in 1941. When his peers began lighting their stadiums in the '30s as a way to pump up interest in the game in a faltering economy, Cubs owner P. K. Wrigley planned to install lights at the park before the 1942 season. The light-stands were actually sitting in the ballpark, awaiting installation, when the Japanese attacked Pearl Harbor. As the course of history changed, P. K. Wrigley's plans changed with it. He decided to donate the steel he had acquired for the lights to the U.S. war effort instead.

In the coming years, even as the rest of the stadiums added lights, most teams continued to play many games

during the day. Eventually, though, the proportion of day games dwindled as it became clear that night games produced more revenue—both for the teams and for Major League Baseball. By the 1960s, day games were a rarity—except at Wrigley, of course.

There, at the corner of Clark and Addison, the gates continued to open for games in the afternoon only. Fans who wanted a true taste of America's Game the way it had always been played only had to step inside the gates of the historic park to glimpse the days of the past. That's right, the *days*—not nights.

In the '80s, however, when playoff and World Series games were mostly scheduled at night, TV networks, Cubs management, and Major League Baseball began to increase the pressure to install lights—even threatening to make the club play any postseason games at Busch Stadium in St. Louis.

Finally, much to the chagrin of baseball purists, lights came to Wrigley Field in 1988. At first, only 18 nighttime home games were allowed per season. This number has steadily increased over the years to 30; still, baseball at Wrigley remains mostly a daytime experience.

For the debut of the lights on August 8, 1988, media outlets came from all over the country. The game against the Philadelphia Phillies was nationally televised. And when 91-year-old Henry Grossman—a fan who had attended his first Cubs game in the good old days of 1906—threw the switch, there was light at Wrigley Field.

Alas, there was also a downpour. The game didn't get out of the fourth inning before it was postponed by the umpires. There was far less pomp and circumstance on August 9, but there was indeed night baseball. And the first official night game under the lights at Wrigley Field ended with a Cubs victory, as they bested the New York Mets 6–4.

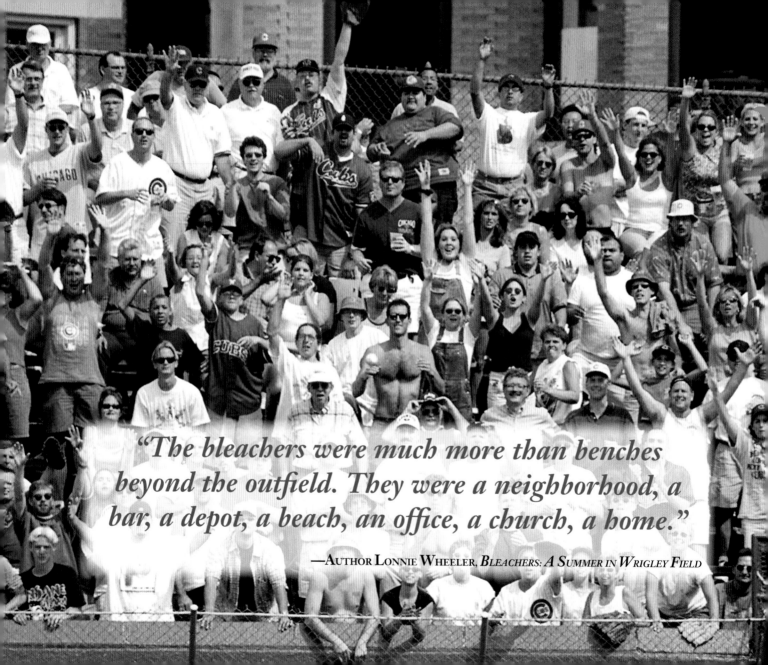

"The bleachers were much more than benches beyond the outfield. They were a neighborhood, a bar, a depot, a beach, an office, a church, a home."

—Author Lonnie Wheeler, *Bleachers: A Summer in Wrigley Field*

THE BLEACHER PREACHER

Jerry Pritikin's father took him to his **first baseball game at Wrigley Field in 1945.** When the Cubs won the National League pennant a few weeks later, dear old Dad told the eight-year-old he was too young to attend the World Series but promised his son he would take him next time.

Pritikin is still waiting. He does not wait idly, however.

Known as the "Bleacher Preacher," Pritikin is a regular at the Friendly Confines. He **wears homemade T-shirts touting the praises of the Cubbies** and carries signs that read "We Believe," "We Have Just Begun to Fight!" or "There are 86 Days 'Til Next Year," a reference to the proverbial "next year" Cubs fans have been waiting for since that pennant in '45.

Pritikin was actually far from Chicago's north side when the "preacher" bug bit him in the 1980s. He was living in San Francisco when he became involved with a local production of *Bleacher Bums*, a play about the fans in Wrigley Field's cheap seats. When it appeared his dream of a Cubs pennant was about to come true **during the division title campaign in '84, Pritikin decided to spend every day of the season's last month in the bleachers.**

Pritikin initially called himself the "Bleacher Creature" but changed it to "Preacher" after learning that the Detroit Tigers had an entire section of fans calling themselves the former. Harry Caray invited Pritikin on the air during a game, Chicago newspapers wrote features about his boisterous bleacher sermons, and Pritikin has been something of a celebrity ever since.

Of course, now in his seventies, he is still waiting and hoping to fulfill a promise more than 60 years in the making.

1989: THE BOYS OF ZIMMER

Cubs fans cherish the memory of every playoff season, and they agonize over the close-call defeats that ended them. The 1989 season, which had many highs but ended with one long, sad exhale, left many fans with mixed emotions.

Coming off a 77–85 finish in 1988 under manager **Don "Popeye" Zimmer,** expectations were low. But aided by the bats of rookies Jerome Walton and Dwight Smith, the '89 Cubs surprised everyone.

Walton stole 24 bases, batted .293, and was chosen National League Rookie of the Year. Smith smacked nine home runs, with 52 RBI, and batted .324 while playing more than 100 games in the outfield. He came in second in the Rookie of the Year tally. Together, they complemented the

solid talents of Ryne Sandberg, Mark Grace, and a young pitcher named Greg Maddux, who won 19 games and carried a 2.95 ERA. Always the consummate professional, Ryno was named to the All-Star team for the sixth straight year en route to winning his seventh consecutive Gold Glove. Not to be outdone, Grace had one of his finest years, batting .314 with a .405 on-base percentage and a .996 fielding average.

Zimmer, a baseball lifer, presided over the mini-circus as the Cubs emerged from the pack and fought for the top spot in the NL East. "What you lack in talent can be made up with desire, hustle, and giving 110 percent all the time," Zimmer encouraged.

By September, everyone recognized that the Cubs were for real and in a key mid-month game, shortstop Shawon Dunston buried the Pittsburgh Pirates with a grand slam. The 7–2 victory gave Chicago a 5½-game lead in the standings with 15 games to play. They went on to win their division by six games over the Mets.

It had been five years since the Cubs had reached the playoffs, and only Sandberg, Rick Sutcliffe, and Scott Sanderson remained from the '84 team. It was also only the second time since 1945 that the Cubs had made it to the postseason.

The Cubs hosted the San Francisco Giants at Wrigley Field in the first game of the National League Championship Series. But things did not bode well for the Cubbies—the Giants crushed them 11–3, smacking around Maddux for eight runs.

The following day at the Friendly Confines, Chicago retaliated with a crucial win to tie

Dwight Smith

the series 1–1. The Cubs topped the Giants 9–5, scoring six runs in the bottom of the first. As it had been all season, it was also very much Grace's day. He went 3-for-4 with two doubles, contributing four RBI to the victory.

In Game 3, the Cubs briefly led 4–3 in the top of the seventh but lost after the Giants scored two in the bottom of the inning. The next day, the Cubs tied the score 4–4 in the top of the fifth, but the Giants took the lead for good in the bottom of the frame. The Giants polished off the Cubs in Game 5 with a 3–2 win. The Cubs had kept it close but couldn't prevail, partially because Giants first baseman Will Clark batted .650 in the series, one of the greatest NLCS performances of all time. The Cubs and their fans would have to keep waiting (and waiting and waiting) for that elusive pennant.